STRANGE
NEW
RELIGIONS
LEON McBETH

REVISED EDITION

Broadman Press/Nashville, Tennessee

© Copyright 1977 • Broadman Press.

4218-06

ISBN: 0-8054-1806-7

Dewey Decimal Classification: 290

Subject Headings: SECTS//RELIGIONS

Library of Congress Catalog Card Number: 76-47780

Printed in the United States of America

PREFACE

The idea for this book originated in the fall of 1975 when I was invited to speak to the "Wives Only Club" at Southwestern Baptist Theological Seminary. That charming group, whose husbands are students at Southwestern, wanted to explore "strange new religions." This gave birth to the title as well as the content of this book.

During the meeting the young women did me the honor of being interested, asking thoughtful questions, and sharing some of their own encounters with strange cults. During the intermission several of them asked about the possibility of these descriptive sketches being published.

Later that fall Johnnie Godwin of Broadman Press visited the campus. In his usual direct way he asked, "Leon, what if anything are you writing these days that might be worth publishing?" After hearing the outline proposal of this book he said, "Sounds like this might meet a real need. Let me think on it. You will hear from me." And I did.

So many people have helped in this project that I cannot thank them all here, much as I would like to. I am grateful to Southwestern Seminary for allowing me a brief respite from teaching duties while completing this manuscript. The staff of Fleming Library, especially Cecil White, went all out to help me obtain materials on each cult.

My students also helped, asking the right questions and suggesting insights and resources. I am particularly grateful to Michael McAleer, Ph.D. candidate in church history at Southwestern, who

69193

has worked this year as my research assistant. He helped locate and research material on several of the cults. He also read portions of the manuscript and made suggestions which doubtless would have improved the book if I had followed more of them. You can thank Marie Skaggs, as I gladly do, for expert typing of the final manuscript. However, much as I appreciate the help of these and many others, any faults in the book must be laid at my door alone.

My family has been unfailing in their encouragement. No words can express my love and appreciation to my wife, who is the most convincing argument I know against the Krishna doctrine of marriage. I dedicate these pages to our three children, Ruth Ann, Mark, and David, all teenagers. Theirs were the faces before me as I wrote. My hope is that these sketches will help them, and others like them, understand better the confusing smorgasbord of new religions today.

HARRY LEON McBETH

Southwestern Baptist Theological Seminary
Thanksgiving, 1976

Preface to Revised Edition

I am glad that this little book has been well-received. As it goes into this second printing, I have taken the opportunity to make certain alterations in the text. My hope and prayer is that future readers will not only understand the new religions better, but will also have a new understanding and appreciation for the Christian heritage.

CONTENTS

1. The Unification Church   7
The Korean Christ: Sun Myung Moon

2. Krishna Consciousness   28
New Markets for an Old Product

3. Children of God   47
Storm Troopers of the Jesus Movement

4. Zen Buddhism   63
Looking Through the Third Eye

5. Astrology   79
Control from Outer Space

6. Transcendental Meditation   94
The McDonalds of the Consciousness Smorgasbord

7. Confronting the Forces of Evil   109
Satan, Demons, and Witches

8. Understanding the New Religions   127
Probing Beneath the Surface

1. The Unification Church

The Korean Christ: Sun Myung Moon

Jesus Christ meant well, but unfortunately he was a total failure. He was sold out by John the Baptist and was crucified before he could accomplish his mission. Jesus was able, however, to salvage at least something from his fiasco—he provided spiritual (but not physical) salvation. The problem began with our original parents in the Garden of Eden, when seductive Eve committed adultery with Satan. By this act Eve was stained with "Satanic blood," and later she seduced unsuspecting Adam and passed this "spiritual VD" to him. As children of Adam and Eve, the whole human race has the literal blood of Satan running in their veins.

To save mankind by blood purification, Jesus came as the second Adam. But before he could marry a perfect wife and have perfect children, the cross wrote on his life, "mission unaccomplished." After two thousand years of mourning, God decided to send a new messiah, the LSA (Lord of the Second Advent), to complete the task Jesus bungled. This Adam III will come from "New Israel," which is Korea. In fact, he is here now, born in Korea about 1920. He will be revealed in these climactic last days, when the world will face an apocalyptic showdown between the forces of Abel (democracy) and the forces of Cain (Communism) at the thirty-eighth parallel dividing North and South Korea. Actually, the messiah's identity is already known: he is none other than Sun Myung Moon himself! Church leaders are careful, however, not to say so in so many words.

No, this is not a put-on. These are but a few of the strange beliefs of the Holy Spirit Association for the Unification of World

Christianity, better known as the Unification Church. It was formed in Korea in 1954 and since 1972 has made amazing inroads in the United States. Its followers accept Moon as messiah, Revealer of Divine Truth, and Lord of the Second Advent. The religion is a strange blend of Christian vocabulary, Oriental dualism, pop sociology, spiritualism, and ancestor worship, bound together by traditional Korean messianism. Moon's followers, often known as "Moonies," have a fanatic loyalty to the Korean "True Father" unmatched in religious history since the early days of Mohammed.

The Unification Church fights Communism, but its members give up all their possessions and live communally. Its teachings make a holy sacrament of marriage, but it disrupts families and severely alienates young people from their parents. It claims to be a religion of the new "Completed Age," but marriages are arranged for its members as in the ancient Orient. Its messiah may ask his disciples to drop out of school, saying, "I am your brain. My word will be law." Moonies are promised that someday they will enter the kingdom of God; but meantime, they continue fund-raising fourteen to sixteen hours a day and turn in all the money to "True Father," whose holdings now approach fifty million dollars.

Who is this dapper deity from the East, and what is his strange appeal in the West? This chapter will try to throw a little light on this ambitious Oriental who is named for both the sun and the moon.

New Moon Over Korea

Sun Myung Moon, whose name means "Sun Shining Moon," was born January 6, 1920, in North Korea. He grew up in the Presbyterian Church, but was later excluded for heresy and gross immorality. Always a mystical and religious youth, as an adolescent Moon claims he had a religious experience in which Jesus Christ appeared on Easter Sunday, 1936, saying, "I am Jesus who came 2000 years ago. My mission still remains to be accomplished. In order to realize God's will, you must be responsible for a great mission." [1]

From that time Moon had frequent conversations with Jesus and other great leaders such as Moses, Buddha, Confucius, and Mohammed. From them he learned that all the great world religions are true, but incomplete. In these last days Moon has been chosen to unify all religions and all mankind and to complete the task begun by others.

Moon was active in underground Korean Pentecostalism in the 1940s and apparently ran afoul of the law because of their strange practices. He attempted to form his own church in 1945, but had the bad luck to locate in Pyong Yang, shortly to become the Communist capital of North Korea. Moon was imprisoned by the Communists from 1946-1950, his followers say for fighting Communism. Others, including a Korean officer in prison with him, claim Moon was imprisoned for creating "social disorder" by claiming the imminent coming of a Korean messiah. Moon regarded the imprisonment as a time of purification.

After his release from prison by U.N. troops, Moon spent several years receiving revelations and studying religion with various Korean holy men. One of the long-standing traditions in Korean religion is that a latter-day messiah would arise in that land and unify the world. Through the centuries many have claimed to be that messiah. Even now Moon has a number of rival messiahs in Korea, some of whom have a larger following than his own. However, Moon is the only one who has successfully outgrown Korea and gotten a foothold in the Western world. For six months he studied with one of these messiahs, Pail Moon Kim, who probably made substantial contributions to Moon's thought. Particularly, the practice of *pikarume*, or blood contamination, so basic to Moon's system, is thought to come from Kim.

In 1954 Moon formed the Unification Church in Seoul. Followers wrote down his teachings, which were in print by 1957 under the title *Divine Principle*. He presently claims over 500,000 adherents, but others calculate nearer one-tenth that number.

Whether for its influence or affluence, Moon determined to expand to new markets in the United States. His system gives

America a large place in prophecy. After several trips to this country, he got his first attention as sponsor of the Little Angels, a Korean girls' choir. The Little Angels were a big hit, and through them Moon met President Eisenhower. Miss Young Oon Kim, who came to the United States in 1959 as a student, first introduced Moonism to American students. In 1972 Moon launched his American "One World Crusade" (OWC), with giant "Day of Hope" rallies in seven American cities. The next year he held rallies in thirty American cities, with intensive media publicity. His giant Madison Square Garden meeting in 1974 and Yankee Stadium rally in 1976 further popularized his movement in America.

From having only thirty young followers in 1972, the Moon cult has grown to perhaps three to five thousand committed disciples in this country, plus a larger number of sympathizers. The "signed members" are gathered into perhaps 125 centers or communes around the country. Moon now has "witnesses," or missionaries, in 123 nations. So far his greatest success has been in Korea, Japan, and America, with considerable interest in West Germany.

One fascinating fact about this church is its rapid accumulation of vast wealth. Neil Salonen, president of the American branch, said, "In 1975 we received nearly twelve million dollars in cash at our national headquarters in New York City. But the total collected all over the country was much larger." [2] If reports of ex-Moonies are correct that the cult consistently underreports its collections, the amount may be twice that. Moon and his church now own more than twenty million dollars in American property, including several choice estates along the Hudson River north of New York City, sometimes plunking down as much as one million dollars in cash down payments. The sixty-eight-acre international headquarters at Tarrytown, New York, cost two million dollars, and the site of the group's training center, farther north at Barrytown, cost one and one-half million dollars. The cult also owns the valuable Columbia University Club, just off Times Square in the heart of New York City. Moon owns property in all fifty states. His latest purchase was Manhattan's famed Hotel New

Yorker, for over five million dollars. The group is presently reported to be planning to purchase the Empire State Building. Most of this property is tax exempt.

In addition to American holdings, Moon is also a wealthy industrialist. His holdings include South Korea's Il Haw Pharmaceutical Company, which exports ginseng tea, and Tong Il Industries, which manufactures firearms and ammunitions. Some estimate his total wealth at fifty million dollars or more.

How does this strange cult win such fortune and following in America? Clearly, it is not the personality of Moon himself. He is rather unimpressive as deities go, a stocky Korean who speaks no English and is given to wearisome three-hour speeches. Nor can the appeal be in the cult's new scriptures. The *Divine Principle* is a hodgepodge of Christian fundamentalist vocabulary, Taoist dualism, Satanism, and charts from Moon's engineering background, held together with high-sounding but essentially meaningless jargon.

Probably the primary appeal is to be found in the conditions of American society. Whether we call this the Age of Aquarius or some other title, there is a pervasive feeling that the world has ended and we are in a new age. The social upheaval in America since the death of John F. Kennedy has left a generation of youth without an anchor. Traditional values have eroded, and the wars in Korea and Vietnam left American youth angry and alienated. Modern industrial society has severely weakened the American family, revealing the much-publicized generation gap. Some converts find in the commune the family they never knew before, a "warm womb [that] shuts out care, responsibility, and the need to think for oneself." Bitter alienation from parents is so common among Moonies as to be almost their trademark.

Reading the Bible by Eastern Light

Moon religion is a syncretic mixture. Its theology is made from a recipe allowing generous measure of ingredients from East and West, flavored by the mysticism of Moon's own revelations. His own spokesmen say that Moon's teachings "extend the universality of Judeo-Christianity to embrace Oriental concepts of God and man."

The "Bible" of the Moon cult is *Divine Principle*, the record of Moon's revelations. First written down in 1957 by Yoo Hyo Won, it is now available in a radically altered 1973 revision. Questions of belief or behavior can be settled by appeal to the "DP," although the direct word of Moon himself is still the ultimate authority. Moonies read the Bible, but regard it as an incomplete revelation written in symbols which cannot be understood apart from Moon's DP. One of Moon's titles is "God's Cryptographer," since he deciphers the Bible, which has been read for two thousand years but never understood until now.

God, in the UC system, is a syncretistic Oriental deity. Moonie students are taught that "God has Original Sung-Sang and Original Hyung-Sang. This is the essence of Perfect Sung-Sang in His personality." This OSS and OHS mean that God is complete—he has multidimensional reality. He is at once masculine-feminine, inner-outer, positive-negative, and embodies both Yang and Yin.

Moon's favorite metaphor to illustrate God's character comes from his own electrical engineering background, the interaction of positive and negative forces in protons and neutons. A typical passage informs us that "God's essential character and His essential form assume a reciprocal relationship with His 'essential positivity' and 'essential negativity.' Therefore, God's essential positivity and essential negativity are the attributes of His essential character and essential form. So, the relationship between positivity and negativity is similar to that which exists between character and form." [3]

However, it is clear that the real God of Moonism is Moon himself. He is worshiped as God, his followers pray to him, he is known as "True Father," and he can forgive sins. Moon is called God's "lump of truth" and a "faucet of the inexhaustible truth of God" that can be turned on and off as needed. To his followers "Father's words are God's words," and one enthusiastic convert announced that "Father's inside is 100 percent vacant. Then Heavenly Father can occupy 100 percent." Members must give absolute obedience to Moon and be willing and ready to literally die for him or whatever is necessary. Property and family belong to Moon. Followers are reminded that this situation applies to "even a wife or husband—don't think, she is my wife or my husband. Before she is your wife, she belongs to Father."

The fall of man is probably the most bizarre doctrine of the Moon cult. It teaches that God created Adam and Eve and placed them in the Garden of Eden about six thousand years ago. After a time God intended to unite Adam and Eve in marriage and, with himself as third party, form a perfect Trinity of God, man, and woman. But before they were ready for marriage, Eve was seduced by Satan; and by their sexual union she "had a blood relationship with the angel (Satan) through her evil love centered on him." Having become prematurely aware of the delights of sex, Eve in turn seduced Adam, who in turn was contaminated by all the evil Eve had picked up from Satan. The whole human race, therefore, as descendants from this original couple, has "satanic blood" in their veins. The problem of sin, Moonies are taught, is that "the womb of my mother was defiled by Satanic blood" and that "six thousand years of historical fornication came to fruition *in me.*" [4]

Salvation therefore must come by a process of *pikarume,* blood purification. Jesus made a valiant attempt to achieve this, but failed for lack of a wife. After two thousand years of grief, God has now sent another messiah, the LSA, who will marry a perfect wife, have sinless children, and thus finally overcome Eve's folly. If this explains how Moon's children are saved, it leaves a murky explanation as to how others are. In the early years Moon apparently both preached and practiced the doctrine that sexual relation with the new messiah could cleanse the blood. He has been often accused, especially in early years, of holding ritual orgies in his church.

Moon emphasizes the "third Adam." The first Adam was in Eden and the second in Israel, but the third will come from Korea. All the prophecies and proofs so indicate, Moon teaches. Just when the political situation reaches its worst, "New light will appear from the East, showing direction to all mankind," and "the nation of the East where Christ will come again would be none other than Korea," while "the Korean people will become the 'Third Israel,' God's elect." [5] An additional proof, if one is needed, is that the climate of Korea corresponds to the climate of the original Eden.

If God is an Oriental Yin-Yang and man a sexually tortured Freudian misanthrope, Satan clearly plays the lead role in Moon's cosmic cast. He is somewhat like "Big Brother" of *1984*. Moonies speak, write, and apparently think far more of the devil than of God. Satan is used to explain simply everything. People get sick because they have yielded to Satan, collections are low because Satan was in the crowd, converts must not visit parents because Satan is in the parents, True Father gets a bad press because Satan is in CBS, the toilet stops up because of Satan, and Moonies on a high-starch diet become constipated because of Satan.

Satan and various of his evil spirits can invade a person or his possessions, so one is never safe. The ceremonial use of "Holy Salt" can ward off Satan if properly sprinkled in one's room, clothing, or food. When Moonies rent a room, one of their first acts is to see that it is properly "Holy Salted." Cars and bicycles are also salted, with what results one does not know. By prayer ordinary table salt can be turned into Holy Salt.

Moonies are taught that evil spirits not only may possess them, but may imitate others. Your leader's voice on the telephone, no matter how familiar, may not be your leader at all but a clever demon who imitates his voice to direct you into sin. Only True Father is immune, and one can often exorcise evil spirits by repeating three times "in the name of True Father."

Clearly Satan is more than a doctrine or supernatural being in the Moon cult. Although members may not know it, Satan is the primary means of social control in the group. To motivate Moonies to be faithful and to immunize them against defection, leaders appeal to various factors. The appeal not to forfeit their place in the coming kingdom and the reproach not to grieve the loving heart of True Father are major, but by far the most significant factor of social control is fear of Satan and his wiles. Moon could function nicely without God, but the devil is absolutely essential.

Moon bills himself as a Christian, though he teaches that Christianity is done for and that churches with their has-been Christ are living on borrowed time. Christianity, like other religions, has its fragments of truth and helped prepare the way for the new messiah. Now in this "Completed Testament Age" old ideas and messiahs must give way to the new, for "the mission of the Unification Church is to restore the failure of Christianity." [6]

Ancestors show up frequently in Moon teachings, reminding us that this is still an Oriental cult. Good ancestors mean that one will be promoted to high leadership in the Unification Church; bad ancestors mean that you probably won't be saved at all. Bodily infirmities are often explained as due to the sins of ancestors. One convert was told her severe glaucoma was caused by an ancestor who was a peeping tom!

As a former engineer, Moon seems to attach almost magical significance to numbers. Perhaps no modern religion is more caught up in numerology. By arbitrarily assigning theological and prophetic significance to numbers or periods, both in the Bible and in history, Moon is able to "prove" that all of human history culminates in a new messiah.

Anti-Communists Living Communally

The Unification Church opposes Communism to the point of hysteria, but its members' life-style takes pages from the Marxist notebook. While Moon and his family live in opulent Oriental splendor, lowly "workers" subsist on cheap and scanty rations and give all their possessions and earnings to the group. Sometimes as many as twenty-five young men and women may be crowded into a small house with one bathroom.

Like the Krishna devotee, the Moonie's day begins early. After breakfast there is usually a lecture and a sort of pep rally to get psyched up for the day's selling or recruiting on the streets.

The faithful spend as much as fourteen to sixteen hours, from early morning to midnight, soliciting money and converts. A common health complaint of Moonies is foot trouble, from spending so many uninterrupted hours on their feet. The commune director assigns each member his station of the day, a parking lot or busy intersection, and usually makes the rounds in a van to put them out in the morning and again late at night to pick them up. Any spare time is spent in hearing repetitious lectures and in prayer. The prayers are sometimes spoken aloud, with the convert crouched Oriental-style with his forehead banging against the floor. Those who have heard them say that the prayers often have a hypnotic rhythm.

Lectures are fine, and witnessing (recruiting) is important; but the main ministry of Moonies is *raising money*. They make bulk purchases of candy, peanuts, flowers, and small curio items, and hawk them on the street for many times their original price. For example, a thirty-four-cent box of candy will bring about two dollars; but the best profit is in a four-cent artificial flower which will sell for one dollar. Moonies also solicit donations, and people are told the money is to help rehabilitate teenage drug addicts or to provide day care for underprivileged children. Of course, no such causes exist; the money is turned over to the church, and ultimately to headquarters. This may appear dishonest to the public, but Moonies are taught to regard it as "heavenly deception." Any means to get back from Satan what originally belongs to God is not only permissible, but commendable. Moonie converts are also coached in how to appeal to their parents for sizable donations.

Unification members do not merely *offer* items for sale; they *sell.* They are psyched up by prayer and determination before the day begins. There is also considerable peer pressure and rivalry, for a person's sense of worth in the cult is directly related to the amount of his daily take. One "super salesgirl," who had fantastic success even on "one-car parking lots," was described as saying:

"I'm going to have victory for Heavenly Father." She was just determined ahead of time. There was absolutely no doubt in her mind that she was going to claim victory . . . . She would challenge God, she would challenge Satan. She would pray for people to come with money, and she would get incredible things to happen . . . . And it was because she was challenging God and challenging Satan and challenging the parking lot. She challenged everything.[7]

Perhaps the record for aggressive selling goes to the Moonie girl who attempted to sell a ticket to one of True Father's lectures to a lamppost! Boys are taught how to appeal to the guilt of prosperous Americans to get a donation. Girls are taught to use their "fallen nature" (sexual wiles) to loosen the pocketbook. A seductive smile and a hint that it would be nice to meet later can bring in a few more shekels. However, girls are cautioned never to go anywhere with men in promise of a donation; and if any man makes improper advances they are to "cry, bite, roar like a lion." If a man attempts to kiss a Moonie girl, she is instructed to bite off his tongue. Perhaps the most distasteful assignment for young women is to go into bars near midnight and flirt with drunks to raise their daily quota of money.

The average daily take is reported to be about 150 dollars, and practically nobody falls under 100 dollars a day. The really good ones take in 300 to 500 dollars a day. All of this money is faithfully handed over to the leaders; at least, there is no record of holding out on True Father. Some communes also run legitimate businesses such as ice-cream stores, fast-food outlets, and farms. Some of their ventures are at least partially funded by the government, and many Moonies live on food stamps. Despite receipts that can run well over 1000 dollars a week, they are technically unemployed and have no income.

Next to fund-raising, recruiting new "spiritual children" is the Moonies' major activity. "Would you like to join the Unification Church?" would be the *last* thing an alert Moonie would say to a prospect. Under Korean tutelage the Moonies have reduced recruitment to an art. They seek young people from the middle and upper classes and are particularly active on and around college campuses. By personal invitation and by newspaper ads, they invite young people to a weekend seminar of fun and fellowship "to discuss how we can better ourselves and others."

Many young people, new on campus and already a little homesick, are attracted to a modestly priced weekend in the country with attractive and friendly young people, especially if a few seductive smiles are thrown in. There is no mention of Moon, the Unification Church, or religion in this initial contact. In response to direct questions, Moonies will deny that they are from the Unification Church. This answer may have a shadow of truth, for most of these training sessions are conducted by one of the more than forty front groups operated by the church. Recruiters often tell a prospect and his family that the group is much like the Peace Corps.

Later, after the prospect is "love-bombed" with friendship, flattered, and courted, he is allowed to discover that this is a religious group. As the 3-day session ends, he is invited to remain for the 7-day session; and about half do. Those who join continue to subsequent sessions of 21 days and 40 days, and the most promising are sent to the seminary in Barrytown for the 120-day training course.

Like selling, witnessing is done aggressively; and "spiritual children" are tallied up like scalps. Girls, especially the Koreans, are encouraged to cook delicacies from their country and invite prospects to dinner. Boys are taught to start an argument because collegians seem impressed with those who can outargue them. Students are taught "to smile and to really be sincere and to really be aggressive . . . and absolutely determined." No more than three minutes are to be devoted to one person unless he shows interest. Moonies are reminded to witness when they go to the rest room, and and the greatest compliment is to "become like a witnessing machine." One young man testified that he pursued a prospect up the ladder of a water tower to witness to him.

Perhaps sensing that his time may be short, in 1975 True Father introduced a new quota for winning converts. By a program called "Pioneer Witnessing," each member is assigned to bring in three new members a month. The cult has been more successful in raising money than in winning the numerous American disciples that True Father needs and that his scriptures predict. Therefore, there is redoubled emphasis on winning new converts and guarding those they already have.

The training of new converts is one of the most controversial aspects of the Moon cult. Parents and ex-members accuse the cult of massive brainwashing, mind control, and personality erosion. Psychiatrists who have examined ex-Moonies almost uniformly find them to be empty, vapid robots who are at best "mentally sterile" and at worst candidates for mental institutions. Practically all ex-Moonies require hospitalization to get their bodies on an even keel again, and over half require psychiatric care as well. The emotional recovery rate is far from 100 percent.

The world first heard extensively of brainwashing in connection with our POWs in North Korea, the exact area where Moon put his system together. Converts are drilled by endless hours of repetitious lectures, with no questions allowed. They are so programmed that Moonies in New York and San Francisco may say the same thing, in the same words. They are under continual fatigue, with at least nineteen hours a day programmed for them; they have no free time. Mail rarely reaches them, and they are never alone with time to think. Their low-protein diet leaves them constantly hungry and malnourished. Powerful symbols of True Father, Satan, and True Church are used to keep them in line. Moon frankly tells his followers, "I am your brain," which allows them to discard their own.

The result may be a group of robots with smiles that appear painted on and eyes that look like something out of a horror movie. They say their spiel crisply, but even a layman can tell that their minds are out to lunch.

Psychiatrists who appeared before a group of senators and congressmen in Washington in 1976, on the basis of interviewing about 150 ex-Moonies, cited the group as a definite hazard to mental and emotional health, particularly in the eighteen-to-twenty-two age group. They said, "We definitely believe

that brainwashing, mind control, persuasive coercion is occurring
. . . . The technique used in brainwashing is exactly the same,
whether it be Reverend Moon's Unification movement, whether
it be the Hare Krishna movement, whether it be anything else." [8]

Former members are unanimous in their belief they were brain-
washed. Their letters, many of them presented to the government
hearing described above, speak of becoming mental and emotional
captives. "They completely ripped off my mind and my free will,"
said a twenty-one-year-old New York girl. "I was a robot for
Moon. My mind was empty. It was just a reflector of everything
they told me." [9] Parents agree and grieve to see formerly bright
young people come home with minds so muddled they cannot
decide whether to go to the bathroom without being told and
agonizing whether or not it is God's will.

Marriage and sex among the Moonies is quite different from
Hometown, U.S.A. Marriage is perhaps the central core of the
Moon system, and is the nearest the church has to a sacrament.
Bad sex practices led to original sin, and there is no salvation
apart from proper sex practices. Somewhat like Mormons, Moon
teaches that "true marriage" (that is, marriage between members
of the Unification Church) is for all eternity. Marriages of non-
members are not considered valid, but are mere license for adultery. These marriages do not continue beyond this life. In fact,
members who were married before they join may be separated.
Years ago in Korea numbers of men became converts because
Moon assigned them new wives! New converts who are allowed
to remain married must abstain from sex for at least seven months.

Single members who wish to marry have a mate chosen for
them. They may nominate four or five prospects who would be
acceptable, but their mate may or may not be chosen from these.
Local leaders screen the pairings, but only Moon can confirm
marriage choices. Some admiring followers boast that Moon is
so insightful that he can just glance at people and assign marriage
partners in less than thirty seconds.

Newly married couples must abstain from sex for forty days
because Christ was tempted for forty days in the wilderness. They

must not use birth control, for "you should have as many children as possible. One, three, five, even a dozen or more children are no problem." Since such children are sinless, as was Jesus, if all Moonie couples would follow this practice, soon there will be "hundreds of Jesuses living on earth."

Moonie marriages are not always by couples. Sometimes mobs are married at once in a giant wedding ceremony. In Seoul in 1970 Moon united 777 couples, some of whom had not met before that day. Some observers think Moon uses marriage between Americans and non-Americans to avoid deportation of militant missionaries who are in this country illegally.

Which Kingdom?

While Moon preaches the kingdom of God, close scrutiny shows that he is deeply interested in politics. He has for years been a major political force in Korea, and recent evidence indicates that this alien to our shores has had a surprisingly large influence in our own government. Moon's political activities have focused an increasingly critical eye upon his cult and may yet be the means of doing them in in America.

The Moon system evolved out of the seething caldron of Korean politics. Dominated during the first part of this century by Japan, Korea was later brutally slashed in two by the Communists. To many Koreans, including Moon, the nation appeared in a "Suffering Servant" Christ role, and the thirty-eighth parallel seemed the ultimate confrontation between God and Satan. Moon's super-patriotism and his dogged last-ditch support for President Nixon attracted widespread attention. He repeatedly preached that "God loves Nixon. God chose Nixon to be president. Nixon must remain president." At one meeting he reportedly kneeled to the president. The fall of Nixon is definitely a factor in the rising tide of opposition against Moon in America.

In the 1950s Moon was kicked around some by the Korean government, but in recent years he has become a favorite of the Park Chung Hee regime. While legitimate Christian groups have been sorely persecuted by this oppressive government, Moon is almost part of the government. His interpreter, Col. Bo Hi Pak, is a former official in the Korean CIA and is under investigation by a House subcommittee in Washington. There is growing evidence that Moonism has made extensive and successful efforts to influence the American government.

One of Moon's major political goals has been to assure continued American support for South Korea. There is reason to think the Korean government has helped fund Moonie efforts to influence Congress. If this charge, which is presently under investigation, proves true, it will raise questions about Moon's legal status as a resident alien in this country.

The Freedom Leadership Foundation (FLF), one of the dozens of front groups for the Unification Church, is a lobby group based in Washington. A communiqué from top church leaders announced that "Master needs many good-looking girls. He will assign three girls to each Senator. That means we need 300. Let them have a good relationship with them. One girl is for the election; one is to be the diplomat; and one is for the party. If our girls are superior to the Senators in many ways, then the Senators will just be taken by our members." [10]

However, Master did not get three hundred. The Washington lobby is staffed with about twenty-five crack troops who have apparently had fantastic success in infiltrating the offices of legislators and influencing laws passed on Capitol Hill. They roam the halls of Congress and spend hours lobbying, though for a nonprofit, tax-exempt group this is clearly illegal. Individual Moonies are reportedly assigned to influential members of Congress. Their job is to win the confidence of their assigned legislator and seek to win approval for projects favored by the Unification Church. Some of these have proven to be persistent and able lobbyists.

One FLF member who later defected gave the following testimony before Sen. Robert Dole and a congressional inquiry in early 1976:

In August of 1975 I was sent to Washington, D.C. at Moon's personal request to do public-relations work on Capitol Hill for him and for South Korea. The Washington P.R. Center has approximately 20-25 young men and women working full-time in this capacity. I, like all the others, was assigned a list of Senators and Congressmen which were to be my own contacts exclusively. P. R. members were to make gradual acquaintances and friendships with staff members and aides and eventually the Congressmen and Senators themselves, inviting them to a suite in the Washington Hilton, . . . where dinner and films or short lectures on Moon's ideas would be presented. All this effort is sort of an ongoing program by Moon to get political support for himself and the Park Chung Hee dictatorship in South Korea.[11]

Former members of this lobby group have testified that they have seen bills come out of Congress that not only supported their positions, but *used their exact words.*

Moon's own political statements are ominous. At various times he has said:

If the U.S. continues its corruption, and we find among the senators and congressmen no one really usable for our purposes, we can make senators and congressmen out of our own members . . . . You [Unification Church] would determine who would become senators and who the congressmen would be . . . . We can do anything with senators and congressmen; we can influence them . . . . We could control the government . . . . The whole world is in my hand, and I will conquer and subjugate the world . . . . The present U.N. must be annihilated by our power. We must make a new U.N. Then, I must be able to make out of you world-renowned personages . . . . The time will come, without my seeking it, that my words will almost serve as law. If I ask a certain thing, it will be done. If I don't want something, it will not be done . . . . We have fifty states. And within 120 days, all the state representatives can be changed. That means we finish three terms and then all the state representatives can have our training.[12]

From these and many similar statements it is clear that Moon's ultimate goal is nothing short of actually taking over the United States government. That is quite ambitious, even for a messiah.

Rising Tide of Opposition

Because of its commitment to religious liberty, America has been tolerant of the swarms of swamis and gurus who have set up shop here. However, one senses a groundswell of protest, anger, and backlash against groups who are clearly financial and emotional rip-offs, with Moon's group bearing the brunt of opposition. Parents led the protest when they saw how Moonism destroyed their young people. At last American religious leaders are becoming aware of Moon's incredible doctrinal teachings. There have been many calls to investigate Moon's ties to the Korean CIA; efforts to influence American internal affairs, tax exemptions, violations of minimum-wage laws, illegal immigration; and the possible use of arranged marriages with American citizens to avoid deportation of Moon missionaries. Even Moon's own status as a permanent resident alien is under review.

One feature of the cult is the bitter alienation it usually brings between parents and children. Moon leaders recognize this fact and coach their converts in how to pacify parents. In a "sharing meeting," one Moonie said, "When I joined the Unification Church, I didn't go back to my physical parents for almost seven years. My father was sick . . . . He couldn't even move because of sickness, but he came and talked to me and we quarreled and he went back. He cried, and with red eyes he went back. Even afterwards, he wrote many letters and said, 'Come back'—because he was dying. I never, never went back because I had faith." [13]

To rescue their children, some parents have employed Ted Patrick, a specialist in "deprogramming." Sometimes parents have resorted to duplicity and even kidnapping, holding young people against their wills long enough for Patrick to deprogram them. Patrick charges up to three thousand dollars for a successful deprogramming, and a description of what he does sounds almost as gross as what the Moonies do. These methods also raise questions about violation of civil rights, especially if the Moonie is of legal age. Several Moonies have lodged charges against parents for kidnapping, and at this writing Patrick is in legal trouble for his activities.

Most of the deprogrammings have been successful, such as that of a Fort Worth debutante from a prominent family, who was lured home under hopes of converting her brother. Her family changed all the locks on the house to prevent her from escaping and at times physically restrained her. Her deprogramming was successful, and she received nationwide publicity. She is now active throughout the country in seeking to rescue other victims of the cult.

Moon's press has turned unanimously sour. From 1972 to 1974 the media did more than the missionaries to spread the faith and create goodwill for the cult. By 1975 the wind shifted; and major magazines, newspapers, and television began to expose the "dark side of Moon." An unlikely antagonist, Rabbi Maurice Davis of New York, launched a nationwide and increasingly successful campaign to educate Americans about what Moonism really stands for. Rabbi Davis was given a standing ovation when he said before a Congressional inquiry, "Senator Dole, ladies and gentlemen, the last time I ever witnessed a movement that had these qualifications . . . was the Nazi youth movement, and I tell you, I'm scared." [14]

This meeting came about when fourteen thousand parents in Kansas petitioned their senator, Robert Dole, to launch an investigation of Moonism. Forty-two House members and thirty-one senators joined in the inquiry. Senator Buckley of New York was particularly interested because his nephew had recently been rescued from the cult. About four hundred persons, including senators, congressmen, officials from various government agencies, about 150 parents, several former Moonies, and a contingent of present members convened in the Senate Office Building in Washington on February 18, 1976, in what was billed as "a Day of Affirmation and Protest." Testimony was given about the financial, political, and brainwashing activities of the Moon religion. While the response of government leaders was rather vague, there was general consensus that Moonies were using religious liberty as a cloak for illegal activities. While stressing adherence to complete freedom of *religion,* participants called for investigation of the cult's extrareligious activities. Perhaps more important than what the hearing actually did was the resulting public response around the country. There was near-unanimous approval, with a rising chorus of calls, some from high places, for a closer look at the Korean messiah.

Former Moonies know best how difficult it is to leave the cult, and many have testified about the psychological and sometimes physical coercion to keep them. Former Moonies have formed several groups to help other victims find freedom and to assist with their rehabilitation. The most popular of these are IFIF (International Foundation for Individual Freedom), CERF (Committee Engaged in Reuniting Families), and CEFM (Committee Engaged in Freeing Minds).

A Christian Looks at Moon

The Unification Church is probably the most dangerous psychoreligious cult in America today. Christians would do well to become familiar with the Korean messiah who has captured so many of their youth.

The Unification Church is not a church in any traditional sense, and instead of unity it brings bitter division. Like most cults, it rejects the Bible and substitutes its own scriptures. It rejects the biblical plan of salvation. And most seriously, it rejects Jesus Christ and ridicules the cross as a silly blunder. Those who accept its weird teachings on sex will have difficulty forming happy marriages.

Should Christian young people confront Moonies and seek to win them back? In most cases, probably not. As in seeking to save a drowning victim, unless the rescuer is a trained lifeguard, there is a better-than-even chance that the victim and rescuer will perish together. With this in mind, the minister to youth in a Fort Worth church cautioned teenage Christians, "If you are stopped by a Moonie, don't walk; *run* until you are safely away."

References

1. *Unification Church Student's Training Manual* (Barrytown, New York: Barrytown International Training Center, 1975), p. 324. Henceforth cited as Training Manual.
2. L. H. Whittemore, "Sun Myung Moon: Prophet for Profit," *Parade*

(30 May, 1976), p. 7.
3. Sun Myung Moon, *Divine Principle* (Washington, D.C.: HSA-UWC, 1973), p. 24.
4. *Training Manual*, p. 36, emphasis theirs.
5. Ibid., p. 311; *Divine Principle*, pp. 520-21.
6. *Training Manual*, p. 98.
7. Ibid., p. 21.
8. *The Unification Church: Its Activities and Practices*, Part I.
9. Whittemore, p. 7.
10. DAP, Part I, p. 39.
11. DAP, Part II, p. 3.
12. DAP, Part I, pp. 8-9; Part II, pp. 9, 12.
13. *Training Manual*, p. 26.
14. DAP, Part I, p. 40.

For Further Reading

Ellwood, Robert S., Jr., *The Unified Family, Religious and Spiritual Groups in Modern America*. Englewood Cliffs, N.J.: Prentice-Hall, Inc., 1973.
Petersen, William J., "Sun Myung Moon," *Those Curious New Cults*. New Canaan, Connecticut: Keats Publishing Co., 1975.

2. Krishna Consciousness

New Markets for an Old Product

You can see them in any big city, and they stand out like a meteor flashing against a dark sky. Their heads are shaven except for a tiny topknot, and they wear flowing yellow robes slung over their shoulders and tied at the waist. They may be barefoot even in winter. If they are not handing out literature about their religion or soliciting donations, they may be chanting, swaying, and dancing to rhythmic drums. When dancing and chanting their eyes may be closed, and the ecstatic expressions on their faces show they have lost all awareness of earthly surroundings. In the midst of city traffic and busy shoppers, these freakish-looking people chant in Sanskrit, "Hare Krishna, Hare Krishna, Krishna Hare, Hare, Hare Rama, Hare Rama, Rama, Rama, Hare, Hare."

Who are these people, and what do they stand for? Most of them are as American as apple pie. They are *our* young people, who went to our schools and, in many cases, grew up in our Sunday School and church. But now they are members of one of the fastest growing new-old religions in the world. They are devotees of ISKCON, the International Society for Krishna Consciousness. This cult is a split-off from the ancient Hindu religion of India.

Devotees of this ancient cult worship the Hindu god, Lord Krishna, who is sometimes called the Christ of the Indian trinity. Their ultimate goal is to fix their total awareness or consciousness upon Krishna (hence the name of the movement). Total awareness of Krishna will drive out any awareness of anything else—self, others, the world. This liberation from the mundane world of unreality brings bliss.

Most of the converts to this cult are disillusioned youth who are unable or unwilling to cope with daily life, or sensitive youth who are distressed at American materialism and moral decay. Many of them are ex-drug users who found their first escape from the real world via chemical means, but who now find absorption in Krishna a better and more abiding high. They live in separated temples or communes called "ashrams" and follow a rigid discipline of little sleep, vegetarian diet, no illicit sex (and very little licit), and strict obedience to the local "president." Most of the devotees are single, but a few are married "householders"—though husband and wife do not live together. A few are part-time members, weekenders who hold secular jobs through the week and devote their time and income to the movement after work.

A New-Old Religion

Hare Krishna may be strange, but it is certainly not new. This cult originated in northern India in the fifteenth century, a fundamentalist split-off from one of the oldest religions in the world, Hinduism. For generations it survived as one of hundreds, perhaps thousands, of Hindu sects with no more real differences than competing brands of detergent. All of these cults used the same Hindu scriptures and worshiped the same deities, but with slightly different emphases. The Bengali saint Chaitanya, 1485-1527, had a vision that salvation could be obtained by the constant chanting of the name of the adolescent god Krishna, third member of the Hindu trinity. Large crowds followed him as he sang, danced, and chanted. In contrast to most gurus of his day, Chiatanya taught that Krishna was a personal deity, indeed the "Supreme Personality of the Godhead." It was he who introduced the chant which is still used, and he predicted that it would one day be heard in every village and city in the world.

Chaitanya perceived this millenium as the "age of Kali"—that is, violence and anger. Since Kali bears the color of yellow, he required his devotees to wear the yellow or saffron-colored robes that are still used. He also prescribed the shaven head, but left a small topknot so Krishna could more easily jerk his devotees to full attention. The Krishna cult has existed for almost five hundred years, but it was small and largely unnoticed until its success in the media-hungry cities of America in the last decade.

Americans have long been fascinated with things Oriental. The nineteenth-century transcendentalists, especially Ralph Waldo Emerson, introduced Hindu philosophy and religion into American intellectual circles. Thoreau said the *Bhagavad-Gita,* primary Hindu scripture, was one of two books which shaped his life. At the Worlds' Parliament of Religions in Chicago in 1893, Swami Vivekananda spoke briefly but captivated his American audience. In subsequent trips to America he found ready soil for Hindu beliefs.

From the 1920s onward various Hindu sects have flourished in this country. Though all the sects centered around the same god Krishna, they are different "denominations" from Krishna Consciousness. Perhaps the most popular was the WKLF Fountain of the World, near Los Angeles, founded in 1949 by "Krishna Venta," a bearded guru who called himself Messiah and claimed his lack of a navel as proof of his divine origin. However, he had the annoying habit of appropriating the wives of his followers, and two irate husbands set off twenty sticks of dynamite under his chair. Only his false teeth and others' memories of him survived.

The Hare Krishna cult was established in New York City in 1965 by Swami A. C. Bhaktivedanta Prabhupada. At this writing His Divine Grace is still living, and he may go down in history as the founder of a major world religion. Bhaktivedanta was born in 1896 in India, later graduated from the University of Calcutta, and worked in Bengal as a chemical engineer. He was initiated into Krishna worship in 1933 and showed such spiritual insight that his teacher ordered him to devote the rest of his life to spreading Krishna Consciousness in the West through the English language. The engineer-turned-guru spent years in study and preparation. In 1950 he left his wife and assumed the life-style of itinerant holy man. He arrived in New York in 1965 with only seven dollars and a tattered copy of his beloved *Bhagavad-Gita* scriptures.

The bald Bengali faced formidable odds in trying to win a hearing in the midst of the seething sixties. Dressed in his yellow robes, he went daily to Tompkins Square Park in New York City and danced and chanted to his god. Soon he attracted a small band of dropped-out youth, some on drugs, all alienated from American culture. Bhaktivedanta was given a month's rent in a Greenwich Village flat, where he taught his tiny band to wear Indian clothing, cook and eat Indian style, and chant to a god most of them had never heard of before. In 1966 he founded ISKCON, and the religion has been growing ever since.

Public attention was drawn to the new movement when countercultural poet Allen Ginsberg professed conversion and wrote some poetry expounding Krishna thought. Later George Harrison wrote "My Sweet Lord," a Krishna celebration song that shot to the top of the charts. This charismatic swami came to America in desperate times. Shattered and disillusioned youth had been stripped naked of values and beliefs. Krishna seemed to offer a way out, a way of escape, a way to deaden the pain. A few big names joined, and the media mushroomed the vest-pocket sect to national prominence overnight.

Growth in America has also stimulated growth back home. Like a hometown product made good, Krishna Consciousness is now a major sect in India, with beautiful new international headquarters in West Bengal, on the fertile Ganges plain. There are over a hundred centers worldwide, with most major American cities represented. From New York the movement leaped the continent to San Francisco and Los Angeles, and it has spread in the Midwest and the South.

The group publishes an attractive magazine, *Back to Godhead*, circulating over a million copies a month in thirteen languages. In 1972 they formed the Bhaktivedanta Book Trust (BBT) in Los Angeles to publish Krishna books and their authorized version of the Gita.

Ancient Ideas in New Dress

What do the Hare Krishna believe? This question is more important to a Christian than a Krishna devotee, for the latter tends to find his religion in ecstatic experience more than in thoughtful understanding. He would rather *experience* than *explain;* and if his doctrines seem irrational to others, that is no barrier to his devotion. Even so, the Hare Krishna do have doctrines.

Krishna is a Hindu sect and, as such, is based upon ancient Hindu scriptures, values, and life-style. Its ideas of God, man, the world, and the future are Hindu. Though now popularized on both sides of the Mississippi, Krishna remains essentially a religion of the Ganges. The following is an attempt to summarize Krishna's major beliefs.

The Bible of the Krishna movement is the *Bhagavad-Gita*, which is now available in twenty-five different English versions. The Gita, as it is popularly known, is but a small segment of an incredibly vast and incomprehensible collection of Indian scriptures. The Gita, which means "song of God," did not originate as an inspired writing, but as a useful commentary upon other scriptures. Its eighteen chapters are made up of a dialogue between Krishna, the "Christ of India," and his disciple Arjuna. The Gita is in three major sections. The first deals with *karma yoga* (the path of work), the second with *jnana yoga* (the path of knowledge), and the third with *bhakti yoga* (the path of love).

The Gita has contradictory teachings, often side by side; this fact allows gurus of various sects to claim "scriptural" authority for their emphases. Scholars date the Gita from about 500 B.C. though Krishna people claim it is at least five thousand years old. The Gita is the basic authority for Krishna doctrine, conduct, and teaching. However, the individual devotee may not interpret this scripture for himself, but must depend upon the authorative translation and interpretation by His Divine Grace, Swami Bhaktivedanta, whose position of authority is very similar to that of the pope in Catholicism. Only his version of the Gita is accepted; all others are "poison."

Perhaps the key concept of Krishna, as of any religion, is its doctrine of God. That people tend to become like what they worship is amply illustrated in the Krishna cult. Hinduism, somewhat like Christianity, has its own trinity, except that the Hindu deities are three separate gods. They are Brahma (Creator), Vishnu (Preserver), and Shiva (Destroyer). Vishnu has been incarnated at least nine times, sometimes as an animal, sometimes as a man.

The eighth incarnation was Lord Krishna, who has himself been reincarnated numberless times. Krishna is often depicted as a young boy cowherd and sometimes as a child. According to Hindu legend, the child-god was born in a stable; his birth was attended by the appearance of a remarkable star; and he was reared by foster parents to save him from a wicked king. Some have suggested Christian influence upon the emerging medieval Krishna cult, perhaps through the Nestorians, but scholars are not agreed upon the matter.

Krishna is everywhere at once, and he has been born on earth numberless times; so the various figurines used in temples to represent him are all different. Although made of wood, metal, or stone, because they represent Krishna, these figurines *become* Krishna and in a spiritual sense cease to be wood, metal, and stone. "When he appears in such a form, it is no longer considered material," so no devotee need hesitate to worship Krishna's "authorized forms" in the temples.

Krishna can "expand himself" by emanations similar to ancient gnostic ideas. This approaches pantheism, for "Krishna, in other words, means everything and includes everything." One passage in the Gita says, "When you have learned the truth, you will know that all living things are My parts and parcels." People are "eternal fragments of Myself," says Krishna. The distinctions between man and God, between man-God and the world, tend to blur in Krishna thought.

The basic human predicament, according to Krishna, is not sin but ignorance. Captivated by his senses, man has been deluded into thinking that his body and the earth are real, whereas they are merely illusory. This preoccupation with the world of unreality blinds man to God and to his own true self. Krishna does not call upon man to repent but to renounce his egocentric life to find oneness with God. The individual soul, or *jiva*, is part of the Supersoul and eventually, perhaps after millions of lifetimes here on earth, will be reabsorbed into Supersoul and lose its individuality.

Krishna emphasizes that man is a spiritual being, and this approach may help explain its appeal. Members teach that "I am not my body; my body is not I." Thus, what becomes of physical persons is of no great consequence. This is one reason the Krishna cult has never been prominent in social work. They believe their prayers and chanting are helpful to the *real* person, but providing food and clothing for mere bodies is insignificant. "The cause of all disturbance and havoc in the world," they teach, "is this false identification with the body." A Krishna child with a cut finger is comforted by the reminder, "Don't worry about the cut; after all, you are not your body."

What a Christian would call salvation is achieved by chanting the name of Krishna. Chanting is the core of Krishna religion. This is the main activity, the primary form of witness, and is the heart of worship. Chanting "is the cry of the individual soul for the Supreme Personality of Godhead, . . . like the cry of a child for its mother." Chanting can also benefit the casual hearer, for it has a "pure transcendental sound vibration." Chanting will "cleanse the accumulated dust from the heart and lead to the understanding of Krishna consciousness," the ultimate goal of life. The founder, Swami Chaitanya, introduced the chant, saying, "In this age of Kali, the only means of deliverance is chanting the holy name of Lord Hari, Krsna. There is no other way. There is no other way. There is no other way." [1]

Given the desperate conditions of fifteenth-century India, perhaps there was nothing else one could do but chant oneself into merciful oblivion. But surprisingly, the chant has retained its popularity to the present time; and American youths raised in an action-oriented society are learning to chant themselves into hypnotic trances. The purpose of the chant is to focus all attention upon God. This religion is Krishna *Consciousness*. One devotee even begrudged the necessity for the eye to blink occasionally, for in that split second one's vision of Krishna was interrupted.

Converts are urged to follow the example of one super-devotee, who went through the entire chant 1,728 times a day. Chanting guards one against error, serving as "a kind of thermal underwear for the mind."

The Hindu world-view denies reality to the material universe. Krishna people, as do other Hindus, regard the world as *maya*, illusion. Whereas a Christian might object to their ignoring reality to lapse into a dream world, the Krishna devotee is trying to struggle free from *unreality*. He wants to escape this world and his body, to attain the real world of Krishna consciousness. The material world is "of no more significance than rainwater contained in the hoofprint of a cow" because it is not ultimately real. Denial of self and "sense gratification" are essential to spiritual progress. For this reason, "When one is actually elevated in spiritual life, he sees all material things as insignificant . . . . a man in Krishna consciousness sees all the possessions of men as mere garbage in the street, all women as his mother, all living entities as his very self." [2]

Perhaps no Hindu doctrine is more familiar in the West than reincarnation. The Krishna people put great emphasis upon reincarnation and explain most troubles in this life as the result of bad *karma* in a previous life. Likewise, one's status next time around depends upon his present life, for "If we simply live like animals in suits and ties . . . in our next life we may be born into a lower species of life." The nearest thing to a Krishna curse is to say that one will come back as a "stool-eater," a surprisingly widely used imprecation that one's enemies be reborn as worms who exist in feces.

One reason for Hindu vegetarianism is the feeling of kinship with all living things and the feeling that *jiva* (souls) incarnated in animals are not different from *jiva* incarnated in human bodies. Some have been through 8,400,000 incarnations without yet becoming perfect, and Krishna is becoming impatient with them! The idea of another chance in another life may be charming to some, but Krishna has no comfort for a handicapped child or his parents.

"Worldly education," which is largely useless in this world, is completely useless in the next. It does not carry over. Unless one finishes his degree in this life, for example, in the next life he will have no memory of his studies and will have to start over again in kindergarten. But spiritual education does carry over. One can pick up at the point where spiritual progress left off in this life. People who are especially spiritual may be rewarded in the next life by being born into the home of Krishna parents.

The reincarnation theme runs through the Gita. One rather eloquent passage says:

> Worn-out garments
> Are shed by the body:
> Worn-out bodies
> Are shed by the dweller.
> Within the body
> New bodies are donned
> By the dweller, like garments.[3]

Another doctrine of the Krishna movement is universalism. They believe that all religions are good, all scriptures are true, and all deities are valid. Lord Krishna says in the Gita, "Whatever path men travel is my path,/No matter where they walk it leads to me." [4]

Universalism is also expressed in an Indian folksong:

> Into the bosom of one great sea
> Flow streams that come from hills on every side.
> Their names are various as their springs,
> And thus in every land do men bow down
> To one great God, though known by many names.[5]

They regard the major religions as complementary. Thus they say to potential converts that embracing Krishna does not mean rejecting Christ, but only going beyond Christ to the next step in spiritual pilgrimage. Krishna is not a denial, but a fulfillment of Christianity, as Christianity was a fulfillment of Judaism. Though all religions are true, ultimately all Gods must be measured by Krishna; and all scriptures must be harmonized with the Vedic writings.

An Alternate Life-Style

The core of Krishna Consciousness is found not in doctrines but in a distinctive life-style of withdrawal from what most people consider the real world. Whatever the converts may say, their *lives* express an utter rejection of traditional American culture, values, family, and education.

Krishna converts leave their families and band together into communes or "ashrams." Most of these are in cities, but at least one is on a thousand-acre farm in rural West Virginia. The devotees live and eat together; they chant and worship together; and each is nourished spiritually by the group. Men and women (even married couples) are kept rigidly separate and sleep in separate quarters. Life in the temple (worship and living quarters are together) is spartan, stripped of those assorted amenities which many Americans now regard as necessities. Clothing, furniture, food, and etiquette would be quite at home in India, but seem alien to American visitors. However, there is warmth and friendship; and these qualities are intoxicating to fragmented youth who have never known a real family or genuine acceptance.

The heavy sleeper might as well forget about Krishna! The daily schedule in the ashram is demanding, and it begins at 4 A.M. Krishna said that most demons are quiet at that hour, so worship is easier. He is the wide-eyed god who abhors sleep and expects his devotees to do the same. A recent article in *Back to Godhead* said, "A person always engaged in the transcendental loving service of the Lord considers sleep to be his greatest enemy, for it is a waste of time . . . . Sleeping more than six hours in twenty-four means sleeping too much." [6]

They hold up as models some heroes of the faith who slept no more than two hours a night. Some observers think chronic fatigue from lack of sleep helps make the devotees obedient to authority, helps them drop into the hypnotic trance from chanting, and definitely contributes to their liberation from awareness of the world around them. The 4 A.M. "early service" fortunately includes vigorous dancing, which helps banish sleep. Study and devotions fill the time until 8 A.M., when the altar in the temple area is decorated with flowers and incense, and breakfast is offered. All food is first offered to Krishna, who "eats the food by hearing the prayers," thoughtfully leaving the actual food for the devotees to eat. However, having been offered to Krishna, the food in a spiritual sense *becomes* Krishna. By eating such food the devotee is not only nourished physically but also receives spiritual strength, a concept strikingly similar to the Catholic doctrine of transubstantiation.

After breakfast the devotees go out on the streets to chant, evangelize, and raise funds. At 11:30 there is another offering of foodstuffs to the deities. At 5 P.M. the temple is opened again, the deities having rested from 1 to 4 P.M. There is a worship service at dusk and another at 9 P.M., when an offering of *puris* (vegetables, milk, and sweetmeats) is made; and "after this final *aratrika* the Deities finally rest." By 10 P.M. most of the devotees do too.

There is no Sunday in the Krishna week, as every day is for work and worship. However, Sunday is a bit different in that the devotees do not usually work the streets, probably from lack of traffic. Sunday is also the day they encourage outsiders to attend the dusk worship service and hear lectures on Krishna Consciousness.

Like all Hindus, the Krishna people are vegetarian. In the Gita Lord Krishna himself said he would accept offerings of "fruit, grain, and the leaf," and his people follow suit. They also rigidly forbid alcohol, drugs, tobacco, eggs, and soft drinks. They do use milk sparingly; in fact, they make it a point to take all food sparingly, eating just enough to stay alive. They explain homely children by saying that their parents ate meat or that the child ate meat in a previous life.

Krishna worship is part of daily life. The temple altar is usually adorned with flowers and holds various figurines that represent Krishna in his different incarnations. These are referred to as "the Deities." The devotees dance, sing, and chant before the deities. Their worship service is active; everyone is involved. Sometimes they swing the deities in a little swing (Krishna, the child-god, is also sometimes called the god of play), and sometimes they place the deities in a little cart and push them around in a sort of procession. One observer described a temple as looking "like a rich kid's dollhouse."

In its new American setting Krishna has been pushed into some un-Hindu practices. Unlike Hinduism generally, Krishna people eagerly seek new converts. Recently they purchased and adapted three buses as "rolling temples," staffed with trained devotees who tour the country seeking converts. They offer classes at the temples (for which there is no charge) and invite interested prospects for meals. Much of their evangelism is by means of literature, from pamphlets to books. They also try to minimize their differences from Christianity, so as not to alienate potential converts. Occasionally they have invaded churches to engage in polemical shouting matches, but this is rare. At times they have been accused of using force to prevent people from leaving, especially children. A widely publicized news story in 1976 told about a father's unsuccessful effort to find and rescue his thirteen-year-old son, who had allegedly disappeared into the Krishna underground.

Like other new cults in America, Krishna undermines the traditional family. The ashram replaces the home and family. Married couples are separated, though living in the same building, and children are taught to regard all adults as their parents. Parents who can afford it send their children away to *Gurukula* (boarding school) and visit them only once a year. In the Dallas Gurukula a little six-year-old girl looked longingly at a visitor and asked, "Are you my mommy?"

Women have a distinctly inferior status in Krishna. Indeed, how could it be different in a Hindu cult? There are twice as many men as women who join the movement, a fact easily explained by the fact that men are more intelligent. Krishna women are taught to be "kind, compassionate wives and mothers." One Krishna spokesman said, "Women need guidance like children. They're innocent and have to be protected . . . Girls are inclined toward cooking and sewing."

Women, we are told, could never become temple presidents

or teachers of Krishna Consciousness. This cult also accepts the ancient idea that black people, by virtue of their skin color, are best fitted for a servant role. There are very few blacks in the movement. A system to escape the world will have little interest for people who have struggled so long to share in the world.

Nobody could be more deathly afraid of sex than the Krishna people. To them sex is the greatest possible evil, the primary barrier to spiritual progress. Sex handicaps us by making it difficult to see that our bodies are not real. One devotee said, "Whenever I think of sex pleasure I spit at the thought." Lust drains off spiritual energy as nothing else does. All devotees, even little children, take two cold showers a day to escape sexual thoughts.

"Sex life, being the apex of pleasure in the material world, is therefore the number one reason for staying in bondage," they warn. One reason for the loose robes is to conceal the bodily form and avoid lust. Little children are taught to be celibate before they know what that is. One little eight-year-old girl explained to a visitor that she wore a loose sari "so men won't be attracted to my body." This is an ancient obsession, for Lord Chaitanya himself said, "We are shackled by iron chains which are beautiful women. Every male is bound up by sex life; and therefore, sex life should be controlled."[7]

Though Krishna prefers its devotees to remain single, marriage is reluctantly permitted for those who cannot otherwise deal with "disturbances of the emotions." Sex outside of marriage is forbidden, with what success one does not know. Somewhat like medieval monasticism, the constant harping upon the subject by Krishna spokesmen suggests that the problem is not yet under control. The Gita describes Krishna's pastimes with his 16,108 wives, of whom the beautiful Radharani is his favorite, in vividly erotic terms. However, Krishna interpreters have "spiritualized" these passages, much as Christians used to spiritualize the more earthy passages in the Song of Solomon.

To those who insist upon marriage, reluctant permission is given. There is no divorce in Krishna, but unhappy partners can resume the celibate state and move to another commune hundreds of miles away. All marriages are arranged by the leaders. A man (or woman) desiring marriage may nominate prospective partners, but there is no guarantee they will be chosen. In many cases, marriage partners have never met before their wedding day. The marriage ceremony is simple, more a pledge of fidelity to Krishna than to each other. Reports say the matchmaking is not arbitrary, that indeed it works like a good computer dating service in matching couples of compatible interests. One pregnant devotee, who had first met her husband the day of their wedding, was asked, "What if the bride-to-be objects to the arranged marriage?" She replied, "A Krishna Consciousness girl is completely submissive. She would never object."

Married couples sleep separately, but once a month they may request permission from the president to have sexual intercourse. This must be at the optimum time for conception, and they must not use birth control. The only purpose for sex is the "union for the sake of procreation of two householders" to produce "nice children to be raised in God-consciousness." Couples must be cautious of their mental states at the time of sex because those attitudes may be transferred to the baby being conceived. Five full hours of chanting and dancing must precede the sex act, which may also help explain its infrequency. Many Krishna wives, like nuns, describe themselves as "married to Krishna."

There are no unwanted children in a Krishna community. Children are prized as new devotees, and no effort is spared to rear them in the faith. In keeping with Hindu tradition, Krishna parents are notoriously lax with their children; and discipline is almost unknown in the earlier years. One mother explained that in Vedic culture "the mother must be very submissive to the demands of her child." Little Lord Krishna himself was quite mischievous and was known to steal honey, play pranks, and pitch tantrums. However, as the child grows older, discipline tightens up; and the adults live anything but undisciplined lives.

Traditional education, according to Krishna, is a total waste of time. What possible good can come from learning to understand a world that does not exist? Worldly knowledge, in fact, makes one "as foolish as an ass."

Although teaching of children takes place in every community that has them, Krishna leaders saw clearly that they needed something more. In 1972 they formed "Gurukulas," or boarding schools for children from ages five through fifteen. The Gurukula in Dallas, for example, has grown from only 3 pupils to over 150. Parents pay a fee of one hundred dollars a month. The children are taught the Sanskrit language, Hindu culture and literature, and Krishna religion. The schools include some math and history, but they are not accredited; and observers doubt the children are getting anything like a functional education. The study of science, as that is generally understood, is strictly omitted. The basic goal is to help the child to self-realization through awareness of Krishna.

Krishna leaders divide their people; and they say that when they win the world they will divide everyone into four basic classes. They are *brahman,* the ruling or guiding class, made up of philosophers and intellectuals; *ksatriya,* the administrators and protectors who oversee the programs devised by the brahman; *vaisya,* the farming, business, and cattle-raising class; and *sudra,* the laborers or working class who are servants to the other classes. A Krishna spokesman said, "This system has been extant from time immemorial, and it will continue through time immemorial. There is no power which can stop it." However, they consider caste based on birth to be degraded. Their modified system, which they claim to be the original, is based on individual ability. Since children are shunted into their slot at an early age, it is not clear who decides who has the qualifications to fit into which caste.

From the beginning the Krishna cult has flaunted its strange customs. As early as 1965 some Americans suggested that if Swami Bhaktivedanta would loosen up a bit and adopt some American food and clothing customs, he would win more converts. He refused, and the very strangeness of the customs probably helped win converts in the early years. However, there is now a decided shift, and some accommodation to American culture is showing up. Devotees who work the streets are now permitted, if they like, to wear customary American clothing and hairstyles.

Nowhere does this gradual accommodation show up more clearly than in photographs of His Divine Grace himself. Early on he was pictured as the typical Hindu guru, with flowing robes, sitting on the floor or having his meal from a piece of wax paper. A recent picture, however, shows him wearing a handsome pull-over sweater, sitting in an upholstered chair at a nice desk, and using electric lights and dictating equipment such as any businessman might use. The room is tastefully appointed and might as easily be the office of a businessman, a college president, or a Protestant clergyman.

This raises the question of culture conditioning. Krishna came here to change America, but may wind up being changed by America. Indeed, history shows that religion is as often the changed as the changer in its interaction with its environment. We may be witnessing the Americanization of Hindu religion.

One major source of funds for the Krishna movement is Spiritual Sky, Inc., their incense factory, which earns nearly one million dollars a year. They also realize considerable profit from publishing endeavors, and new converts usually give their possessions to the movement. The devotees used to sell articles on the street, but more recently they give away the articles and ask for a donation. There is no charge for attending Krishna services or for personal instruction. Despite their large sums of money, there is no evidence that Krishna is designed as a financial rip-off for the personal enrichment of its leaders. In this respect it is quite different from some other religious cults.

Does religious liberty apply to Eastern cults as well as to the Christian denominations? Some people are asking that question seriously. Local authorities in many cities have considered passing ordinances to forbid or restrict cult activities. There have been calls for congressional investigation of some cults, with a view to legislation to control them. In some places Hare Krishna has, as have other cults, encountered legal difficulties in purchasing property.

Despite its official withdrawal from the world, Krishna has shown considerable interest in politics. The founder began promoting his movement in 1965 as an alternative to political leaders of the time. In 1974 Krishna fielded a candidate for the United States House of Representatives on the "In God We Trust" Party. Their political pronouncements show a distinct distrust for democracy, which they describe as "a society of cheaters and the cheated, [where] the biggest cheaters will become leaders." Presently they have no chance to elect devotees to public office, but they are definitely not committed to separation of church and state.

A Christian Looks at Krishna

In seeking to understand this ancient religion in its new form, it is not enough to ask *what* they stand for; it is also necessary to ask *why*. What are the influences which over the centuries have shaped this strange religion of despair? Why do young Americans so eagerly embrace a cult so utterly alien to their heritage?

Although one may confront Krishna in Anytown, U.S.A., he must remember that this cult originated and evolved its teaching in India. Whereas the West has been nurtured by the Graeco-Roman heritage in philosophy and government and the Hebrew-Christian heritage in morals and religion, Krishna comes from a Far Eastern culture where these influences never really penetrated. The philosophies of Aristotle and Plato, the Greek heritage of the importance of the individual, and the concept of democratic self-government are foreign to Krishna. The Hebrew teachings that God created the world and found it good, that God made man and woman for each other, that sexual fulfillment in marriage is one of God's winsome gifts are utterly foreign ideas to Krishna. The "work ethic," sometimes attached to Protestantism but really a part of the larger Christian ethic, is diametrically opposed to Krishna. The Christian concept of ministering to people in need contradicts Krishna. Whereas a Christian would share bread with the hungry, a Krishna devotee would chant to him.

Krishna developed its ideas about food in a land of chronic starvation. Its rejection of sex comes out of a land where centuries of ghastly overpopulation led to disease, degradation, and death.

It is not too difficult to understand how a religion that rejects the satisfying of bodily hungers could develop in an environment where such satisfaction was for the most part impossible. One is reminded of the "beatitude" "Blessed is he who expects nothing, for he shall not be disappointed." Who can say but that, given the conditions of ancient India, rigid control of food and avoidance of sex made sense. However, Hindu teachings (including those of Krishna) have contributed to the modern crises in India, though Krishna people resent one's pointing this out. One is hard put to understand how a set of ideas that have helped lead to centuries of degradation for countless millions of Asians can now be so eagerly embraced in the West.

Perhaps it would help to remember that Krishna is the ultimate dropout. Not having answers to the problems of the world, it becomes easier to dance and chant until the world recedes into dim nothingness. Krishna is antimaterialistic; and in the success-hungry rat race of American culture, Krishna is the ultimate protest. It would be hard to imagine a more thorough rejection of American values and heritage.

Krishna is as close as Hinduism ever comes to Christianity, and that isn't very close. For those who understand neither one, Krishna may appear as a substitute for Christ. But this religion is based on a different Bible, worships a different god, and, whether its young devotees know it or not, offers teachings which at almost every point are a basic denial of Christianity.

By turning inward, Krishna people do not solve problems. They merely ignore them. Chanting and dancing may be fun for awhile, but one cannot chant forever. When the chanting is finished, the world and its problems are still there.

References

1. Damodara Dasa, *The Scientific Basis of Krsna Consciousness* (New York: The Bhaktivedanta Book Trust, 1974), p. 57.
2. *Back to Godhead*, No. 40, p. 19.
3. Swami Prabhavananda, *The Spiritual Heritage of India* (London:

George Allen & Unwin Ltd., 1962), p. 130.
4. Ibid., p. 97.
5. Lowell D. Streiker, *The Gospel of Irreligious Religion* (New York: Sheed and Ward, 1969), p. 37.

For Further Reading

Harper, Marven H. *Gurus, Swamis, and Avataras: Spiritual Masters and Their American Disciples.* Philadelphia: Westminster Press, 1972.
Judah, J. Stillson. *Hare Krishna and the Counterculture.* New York: John Wiley and Sons, Inc., 1974.

3. Children of God

Storm Troopers of the Jesus Movement

An aged bus converted to a camper groans to a stop near a busy city park on Saturday afternoon. About two dozen young people pile off. Some carry guitars; some carry literature to sell or give out; all carry Bibles. The girls mostly wear long granny dresses, wear their hair long and straight, and have a distinctly unkept appearance. The boys wear jeans and T-shirts; some have long hair; and most could merge unnoticed into any city crowd.

They form a circle and strike up a lively tune. Those not busy playing instruments begin a lively, swirling, graceful dance not unlike square dancing. Meanwhile, the dancers' faces flash smiles of joy, and their voices blend in spirited singing. When the dance and music end, the youth fan out among the gathered crowd. They quote Scripture, speak of Jesus' power to save, offer literature for sale, and invite interested youth to come have supper with them back at the commune. Those who accept may never return to home and family again, for these are the "Children of God."

Who are the Children of God (COG)? The question looks simple, but proves surprisingly hard to answer. Parents would like to know, for their teenage sons and daughters have been drawn to COG like moths to the candle. Some have virtually disappeared into a religious underground of Bible-quoting dropouts. Young people, attracted by the Children's sex-oriented literature and "Jesus-rock" music, need an answer before deciding whether to join up and abandon the "Great Whore" (COG's name for America). And increasingly, the law would like to know, for investigation of COG communes has turned up some surprising problems.

One sharp-eyed reporter, after visiting a COG commune, puzzled, "Are these hippie revivalists only what they say they are: an all-volunteer army for Christ, laboring to save us all? Or are they, as more and more detractors insist, brain-washed, anti-American fanatics, fobbing off revolution and hate as the Gospel?" [1]

That question has plagued the Children since their origin in 1968 out of the seamy side of the "Jesus Movement." Are they, despite their ambitious name, more directly the children of American despair and disillusionment? It now appears there is more to COG than has met the public eye. The clean-scrubbed faces presented to the public apparently are not the only faces they have. While speaking of love in public, they have in private taught virulent hatred and strife. Their public speech has been liberally sprinkled with Scripture and "Praise the Lord," but the Children in private retain the obscene vulgarisms of the street. According to sworn court testimony, rape, incest, and polygamy have been taught and practiced by some of the Children and their leaders.

The immediate end of the world is perhaps the main belief of the Children. They firmly believe that theirs is the "terminal generation" and that the "end time" is now. This apocalyptic vision of doom colors their entire system of belief and conduct. They reject American society totally, including its government, churches, schools, families, and especially its jobs. They do, however, accept its contributions of food and money. The Children oppose Communism to the point of hysteria, but they give up all private possessions and live in communes where even the clothing they wear is not considered their own.

This is just a glimpse at one of the strangest new religions in America. This chapter will seek to fill in a few of the details.

Origin of the Children of God

The Children of God are only one of dozens of strange new religious groups to boil up out of the social crises of the 1960s. Their founder is David Brandt Berg, a disillusioned former pastor in the Christian and Missionary Alliance, a small Pentecostal denomination. After being forced out of an Arizona pastorate, Berg vowed to have nothing more to do with traditional churches. For awhile he worked as PR man for Rev. Fred Jordan, a Pentecostal radio (and later TV) preacher in California who sponsored a popular program called "Church in the Home." He also sought to develop his extensive property holdings in California and Texas.

In 1968 Berg and his wife Jane took over a coffeehouse in Huntington Beach, California, that had been established by Teen Challenge. Berg conducted intense Bible-study classes and soon had several young men sleeping at the coffeehouse. This was the nucleus of the Children of God. From a study of Acts 1—5, Berg persuaded the small but intense little group to break all ties with the "system" and live as a commune with all things common. The group included Berg's four grown children and their spouses, who still make up the bulk of COG leadership.

As early as 1965 Berg's mother, herself a street and radio evangelist, had a vision of impending doom for America. This plus the earthquake scare of 1969 led Berg's group, first known as "Teens for Christ," to flee California. Berg had received a vision that the entire state would soon flake off into the ocean. For about eight months the group, numbering fifty, wandered in the Southwest, sometimes reduced (they say) to eating grass to survive.

During their "exodus" the Berg group picked up the name Children of God, and it stuck. They adopted many Jewish features, modeling their commune upon the Jewish kibbutz. The Children took Old Testament names, with Berg becoming "Moses David."

Despite their previous differences, Jordan once again employed Berg in 1970 and allowed the Children to occupy his properties. These included a six-story mission in Los Angeles, a four-hundred-acre ranch in Texas, and a citrus ranch near Coachella, California. This arrangement benefited Jordan in two ways. In addition to their manual labor, which improved the property, Jordan could display the colorful Children on his weekly TV show as a part of his appeal for funds. He was apparently quite successful at this. Critics claim that much of these funds went toward improving his various property holdings.

One of Jordan's properties was a four-hundred-acre abandoned ranch at Thurber, Texas, about seventy miles west of Fort Worth. It was here in 1970 and 1971 that the Children of God reached substantially their present form and attracted the publicity that made them a national group.

From the Qumran Community in Bible times to medieval monasteries, rural isolation has appealed to communal groups trying to escape the world. One could hardly find more isolation than at the ghost town of Thurber. Once a thriving coal-mining area, Thurber has been virtually abandoned since the 1930s. Amid this bleak terrain and searing heat, the Children set up their home commune in a few dilapidated old buildings and scattered trailers. Life was primitive, with two water faucets, no air-conditioning, and an outdoor privy.

In 1971 Berg and Jordan once again split up. The Children vacated all Jordan properties. The Thurber group set up new headquarters in Dallas, and other communes were located around the country. Jordan soon found another youth group to use in his fund-raising.

As the communes multiplied, Berg left more of the direct leadership to his family. These included his two sons, Paul, now deceased ("Aaron"), and Jonathan ("Hosea"), and two daughters, Linda Berg Treadwell ("Queen Debbie"), and Faith Berg Deitrich ("Faithy"). The sons-in-law are John Treadwell ("Jethro"), and Arnie Dietrich, ("Joshua" or "Big Josh"). The elder Berg communicated with the various groups by letters, which came to be known as "Moses Letters," later simply as "Mo-letters." While the elder Berg is still the ultimate authority, perhaps son-in-law Joshua is now the primary on-the-scene leader. The elder Berg is said to be living abroad, perhaps in Israel. Most current COG members do not know the real identity of "Moses" or any of the Berg family.

In 1973 the Children accelerated their exodus out of the United States. Their convictions grew that America was facing a time of "Great Confusion" and that a Communist takeover was either imminent or had already taken place. They twisted biblical prophecies to prove that America was the "Great Whore" of Revelation whom God would destroy. They took pleasure in the crises racking America, singing:

> Three cheers for the red, white, and blue.
> You've turned your back on God,
> Now he's turned his back on you.

One Mo-letter, entitled "America the Whore," said, "It's time for the rape of America, but they're trying to respect her! She doesn't deserve respect: She's an old Whore!" But the final evidence that America was about to be destroyed came in December 1973 with the highly touted "noncomet" Kohoutek. Like other apocalyptic groups, COG went wild in regarding this comet as a fulfillment of prophecy, a proof that the end of the world was near and that America was doomed. Berg dashed off a Mo-letter about Kohoutek, the "Christmas Monster," which he called a "once in ten thousand years visitor" which would light the night sky beyond the brilliance of seven moons. Berg had recently had several visions and had visited the spirit world and "found the spirits all agog about something big that was about to happen." This big event, as it turned out, was the coming of Kohoutek, which would signal "the total downfall of America" and "the end of things as they now are."

Even before Kohoutek Berg had urged his followers to leave America. His scheme of prophecy figured America to be destroyed somewhat before the rest of the world. The Children have a fanatic obsession that America will soon be, or already has been, taken over by Communists. In another Mo-letter in late 1973 Berg said America, like Nineveh, has only another forty days. Therefore, "You in the U.S. have only until January to get out of the states before some kind of disaster, destruction, or judgment of God is to fall because of America's wickedness."

He then gave instructions about how to apply for citizenship in various other countries. Berg had led the way in quitting the United States, and soon major COG headquarters were removed to London and Puerto Rico.

A New Moses

The doctrines of the Children still reflect the Pentecostalism of their founder. Berg led COG to a rigidly fundamentalist interpretation of the King James Version of the Bible, with emphasis upon prophecy, creation of the world six thousand years ago, and a posttribulation view of the millennium. The Children have no formal church or clergy. Their worship services emphasize dancing, singing, and speaking in tongues more than preaching. They also believe in divine healing and demon possession.

They preach a simple salvation based upon acceptance of Jesus Christ as Savior. In no other doctrine are they as true to biblical teachings as in their doctrine of salvation. Most of their witness is a direct testimony of "what Jesus did for me." They do not reflect upon the experience and its meaning, which leads some to question whether the group can survive the first generation of converts.

However, the Children are essentially an end-of-the-world cult. The mainspring of their doctrinal system is the conviction that we are living in the end times, that Bible prophecies point to this as the last generation. Like countless groups throughout history, COG not only believes this, but seems to take delight in the coming destruction of the world and its hated people.

Of course, this is no new doctrine. Throughout history groups have predicted the end of the world on the basis of biblical prophecy or private visions. Usually they seize upon current events to prove they live in the last days, whether it be the French Revolution, the Civil War, or the rise of Adolf Hitler. The Children have seized upon events in the Middle East, such as the rebirth of the nation of Israel in 1948, the Six-Day War of 1967, and the current energy crisis involving Arab oil for their proof.

The Children hold to a version of millennialism known as "posttribulation rapture." They believe the world will be taken over shortly by Anti-Christ, who may be a church leader. Members of traditional churches will capitulate totally to this Satanic figure and renounce their faith. Only the Children of God will remain faithful, and they will be terribly persecuted for a period of years.

From the first the COG has needed outside persecution to maintain its own group identity and hostility to the world.

No one who visits a COG commune could doubt their outward allegiance to the Bible. They memorize huge segments of the King James Version, have Scripture posters on every wall, and listen to Scripture quotations blare from loudspeakers during work, meals, and training times. Each convert wears a leather pouch slung over one shoulder to serve as "scabbard" for his "sword," and the Children can whip out their Bibles at the slightest sign of a prospect or an argument.

While they memorize the Bible, it would not be quite accurate to say they *study* it. They take verses out of context to support their ideas, but remain generally ignorant of the background, languages, and historical situation out of which the Bible came. Consequently, the verses they quote often have no relationship at all to the teaching they use them to support.

After their initial training in Bible memorization, the Children depend more and more on the Mo-letters from Berg. In the Mo-letters Berg gives advice, practical directions, and also shares the "revelations" he gets directly from God or from some place he calls "the spirit world." These Mo-letters clearly assume the place of authority for the Children, who accept them almost on a par with the Bible itself.

Nowhere is the COG spirit more bitter than in their rejection of mainline churches. At first COG members liked to invade churches and shock their staid parishioners with their pronouncements of woe and doom. Besides, they thrived on the publicity, and the churches' rejection confirmed their own validity. Berg scoffed at "church addicts," and his young followers sang:

> O Lord, have mercy on me.
> I hate that damned old sound
> Of the church bells ringing
> And the people coming from miles around.

They describe the church as "a barren old maid of stale religion" and affirm that "You can only get false teaching from a church because it's part of the Whore of Babylon." They sometimes pray that radicals will burn down all the church buildings in America. A Mo-letter on "Other Sheep" said in 1972, "By this time we were so bitter against the churches for their hypocritical do-nothing religion, their multimillion-dollar Gospel entertainment business, and their multibillion-dollar fancy church buildings that . . . we were ready to declare war on the Church System."

But the Children reserve their most intense hostility for the American family. Most groups of the Jesus movement experienced a rather severe generation gap, but the COG reduced it to a major doctrine. They constantly quote Matthew 10:35-37 and Luke 14:26, which they interpret literally to require children to hate their parents. Converts are sometimes called "10:36ers," and the sincerity of one's faith is often measured by the degree of his hatred for parents.

Berg himself set the tone for this in one of his Mo-letters on "Who Are the Rebels?" He said, "You, my dear parents, are the greatest rebels against God . . . . To Hell with your devilish system. May God damn your unbelieving hearts . . . . God is going to destroy you and save us."

Communication with parents is limited. All telephone calls are monitored, and mail is censored. Converts are shifted from one commune to another, and names are frequently changed, so parents find it difficult to trace their children. When they do find their youngsters, they are usually not allowed to speak with them alone. Each commune has a "security system" which enables them to detain, mislead, or otherwise deceive parents. Some COG members have physically assaulted their parents and prayed for God to strike them dead on the spot.

This hatred of family aroused the first serious opposition to COG. As early as 1971 a group of parents formed the Parents' Committee to Free Our Sons and Daughters from the Children of God (FREECOG). Soon thereafter, other parents formed Thankful Parents and Friends of the Children of God (THANK-COG). Some parents claimed their children had been virtually kidnapped into the cult, brainwashed, drugged, and/or hypnotized.

Most of the young people who joined had not had much of

a family life anyhow. This group has always appealed primarily to the alienated, and most of its new converts are either on drugs, alienated from parents, or unable or unwilling to cope with modern life. COG has perhaps the best record of any group in getting addicts off drugs, a fact that won them much of their early favorable publicity.

The Children win most of their converts on the street. When they find someone who appears interested, they literally surround him, quoting Scripture and praying. If the prospective convert tries to leave, they may even use mild physical restraint and pray in a shout for Satan to let go and allow God to save the person. Often they beseige college campuses during exam week, when students are already upset. In some cases, if a prospect seems too adamant, they will practice "smiting," by which they simply crack him over the head with a Bible!

Presently all the members are "joiners." It will be interesting to see in years to come as children grow up in the movement what changes will take place. Significant changes will occur, for theirs is the kind of immediate vision that cannot be handed down to other generations.

Life in the Commune

What is life like in a COG commune? Conditions vary somewhat from one commune to another, but the basic pattern is the same. The visitor can never doubt that it is a *commune*. The Children make no bones about their utter rejection of capitalism, and all goods are shared in common. Most of the members are under twenty-five, so an occasional middle-aged member is an oddity.

All converts take new names out of the Bible. The Children say this helps them assume a new identity for God, but opponents point out that it makes it virtually impossible for parents or police to trace them. The commune is divided, like ancient Israel, into various "tribes" for division of labor. For example, Levi is the tribe of elders and teachers; Zebulon does farming, Simeon food preparation, Reuben grounds-keeping. Issachar is the tribe of mechanics because Is-A-Car sounds suitable, they say with a rare flash of humor. However, since tasks outnumber the tribes, other names have been pressed into service. Thus, Gilgal is the name of the KP crew. Children may swap around from one task to another, but they retain their original tribal membership.

Each tribe has its elders, and the council of elders rules the commune. These elders are not elected; they simply rise to leadership by God's will. Just how God's choice becomes known to the people is not clear. The elder's authority is unquestioned. However, behind the entire movement remains David Berg and his immediate family, who still control the Children of God.

New converts are called "babes' and are expected to spend the first few months in intensive Bible memorization. The convert must give over all his possessions to the group and promise to live by the rules, which include no drugs, no alcohol, no tobacco, no time to oneself, and very little sleep. He is assigned a "buddy," an established member who remains constantly with the newcomer day and night. The new convert's first act in the morning is to awaken his "buddy," with whom he sleeps. All day and all night, while studying, while working, even when going to the bathroom, this buddy is present. The new convert is expected to memorize three hundred verses in the first three months and two verses a day thereafter. Often they write out the verses on scraps of paper and tie them to a cord around their neck, so they can refer to them and repeat them over and over while working. In addition, tapes of Scripture readings blare constantly. For some reason, many Children believe the Bible is more effective if repeated at a shout rather than in a normal voice.

The COG communes have never enjoyed such financial success as the Moonie and Krishna compounds. The COG street peddler counts himself lucky to raise thirty to thirty-five dollars a day, a fraction of what other cults are able to raise. Visitors to COG communes are uniformly struck by the bleak squalor and poverty.

By far the most significant source of income is from the possessions of new converts. Berg said they had to grow to survive. Some converts have cars, stereos, bank accounts, all of which must be given to the group. Converts are also carefully coached in how to appeal to parents for donations. Sometimes the parents are given a subtle hint that a generous donation might result in their learning the location of their child or even a visit home.

In the early years many merchants were sympathetic to the Children, primarily for their work with drug addicts. Some made contributions of money or goods. Each commune has its tribe of "Procurers," whose duty it is to approach merchants for donations of dented cans of food, day-old bread and bakery products, and other surplus commodities. Unlike most of the members, the Procurers are encouraged to have neat haircuts and wear "system" clothes of suit and tie. In recent years Moses David has taught his followers how to qualify for food stamps, unemployment, and other forms of government funding, for, as he said, "We don't turn down anything in the way of help that the governments have to offer." However, "system" jobs are still absolutely forbidden.

Most new COG converts are single, and boys greatly outnumber girls. Marriage is permitted, and there is keen competition "in the Lord" for eligible partners. There is no dating or courtship in the usual sense, but in the closeness of a commune young people work together all day and sing and dance far into the night; so they have plenty of opportunity to get acquainted. A boy who wants to marry will tell the girl he "has a burden for her"; and if she also "has a burden for him," they tell it to the elders. Marriages must be approved by the elders, who sometimes exercise their privilege of substituting some partner other than the one chosen.

The marriage itself is quite a ceremony, lasting for hours, with singing, dancing, speaking in tongues, and prophecy. During the ceremony any boy may stand and say God has revealed to him that such and such a girl is to be his wife. That girl, unless already married, is virtually obligated to come forward and be married on the spot, regardless of her personal preferences. Therefore, what begins as one betrothal often turns into a multiple marriage. In the early days there were no marriage licenses, and for new babies no birth certificates or social security cards, for this would be compromise with the hated "systemities."

Unlike Moonies and Krishna members, married Children have no restrictions upon sexual relations, except they are not to use birth control. They want as many children to be born as possible. They usually practice natural childbirth. When a woman is giving birth, some women act as midwives, while the rest of the women gather around to pray and speak in tongues. Many Children regard physicians as part of the "system" and feel that since most illness is caused by demons anyway, its best cure is through prayer and repentance.

The children of the Children are called BBB's, for Benjamin Bottle Breakers. This is their tribal name, since Benjamin was the youngest son of Jacob. They deliberately break down the nuclear family, so that all children may regard themselves as children of the entire group. Somewhat like the Jewish kibbutz, infants are cared for by women appointed to that duty rather than by natural parents. They proceed from the Infant House to the Toddler House at about age 1, and at about 2 and one-half begin schooling on a modified Montessori basis. Some of the communes use state-approved textbooks, but for the most part the children learn Scripture, hatred for the world, and how to survive in the commune. Observers note that most of the children appear happy and adequately nourished, but dental and orthodontal problems are usually neglected. The Children will, however, obtain and use eyeglasses.

Leaving the commune is not easy, and only about 15 percent of new converts ever do. For one thing, there is more acceptance and warmth than most of the young people have ever known before. Their previous identity is thoroughly broken down and another built in its place. They sleep very little, have long, repetitious Scripture drills, and are subjected to strict discipline by older members. They are never alone and rarely communicate with the outside world except in censored forms. Those who express any desire to leave are harangued and threatened. The Children have a strange "staring technique," by which they stare hypnotically for several minutes directly into the eyes of those who are weakening. Berg claimed that by this method he could literally pull people's souls out through their eyes. Converts with second thoughts are also threatened, not only by what the Children may do, but what God may do. Most are firmly convinced that God would strike them dead if they sought to leave. Those who managed to leave later testified that COG leaders often told horrible stories about ex-members, all of whom met violent deaths. One girl who really wanted to leave Thurber with her father faltered as they reached the gate, screaming, "Dad, if I pass through that gate I'm dead!"

There is no doubt that COG maintains strict mental and emotional control over its members. However, claims that converts are drugged or hypnotized are doubtful. The Scripture drills can be hypnotic for some, and elements of brainwashing are present, though not to the degree one finds in the Moonies and Krishna. However, COG keeps its members on a short leash and makes it difficult emotionally, and sometimes physically, to leave the commune. Those who do leave often have difficulty in adjusting back into society. This is not too surprising when one remembers that their inability to adjust was a major reason for joining COG in the first place. However, ex-Children are nowhere near the mental and emotional cripples that ex-Moonies and ex-Krishnas often are.

Permissive Paradise

In their early years the Children received an almost uniformly good press, but recently people are taking a closer look. Many are shocked at what they find. On September 30, 1974, Louis J. Lefkowitz, Attorney General of the State of New York, issued his "Report on the Activities of the Children of God." This was the culmination of an in-depth investigation authorized by then-governor Nelson Rockefeller. This sixty-five-page report gives sworn testimony detailing the shocking dishonesty, immorality, and vulgarity that marks the inner life of the Children of God.[2]

A fourteen-year-old girl testified that she was repeatedly raped by COG members, who told her it was God's will for her to bear many children for the group. Berg's former daughter-in-law, Sarah, testified that she began to travel with the group when she was fifteen. Paul Berg suddenly demanded that she marry him, and when she declined both Paul and his father subjected her to a constant bombardment of "prophecies" that it was God's will. Frightened, she was forced to have intercourse with Paul in the presence of his father; and later they were married. Later the elder Berg demanded that she have sexual relations with him as well. Just two weeks before the birth of her second child, Paul and his father insisted Sarah have public sex with several of the men to demonstrate methods of intercourse with pregnant girls. When she refused, her husband beat her. Later she fled the commune with her tiny infant, but even after the death of her husband she has not been able to locate or recover her first child.

The Children are certainly not the first radical religious group to undergo change. Some of their extreme hatred, dishonesty, and sexual aberration may have been present from the first, but concealed from the public. Certainly it was potentially present, and perhaps the increasingly permissive attitude toward sex mirrors the personality changes of the leadership.

About 1972 the Mo-letters began to take on erotic sexual overtones, augmented by drawings that by 1974 had become too bold even to be reproduced in newspapers. The letters of Moses David and his wife, Mother Eve, could not be quoted in this book. A 1973 Mo-letter entitled "Come on, Ma! Burn Your Bra," said, "We have a very sexy God and a sexy religion with a very sexy leader with an extremely sexy young following." Another such letter in 1973, entitled "Mountain Maid" and adorned with the kind of pictures ordinarily found in *Playboy*, advocates nudity, concluding: "Can't we leave those summits bare/Without all that underwear?"

In other writings Berg advocates polygamy, concubinage, group sex, incest, and even sex between small children, volunteering that his own first intercourse was at the age of seven. Sex, he said, should be performed publicly like other acts of worship, and he put this into practice by requiring his wife to witness his relations with a young girl who became his "concubine."

Whose Children?

Whether or not Children of God, these people are most certainly the children of America and its desperate decade of despair in the 1960s. Cast upon the restless sea of American disillusionment, these young people witnessed the death of President Kennedy and the Death of God, events which are probably connected. They witnessed Vietnam and the Democratic National Convention in Chicago in 1968. They were fragmented, angry, alienated, frightened, lonely. Most of them have never known the love and acceptance of a real family. No wonder they wanted to drop out and to reject the "system," and even longed for the destruction of a world that had rejected them.

They are repeating history, with some new features. Early monastics also tried to flee the world; medieval followers of St. Francis turned against their parents; and American religious history is cluttered with remnants of groups strikingly similar to the Children. No theme has been more constant through the centuries than belief in the end of the world. Especially during times of stress in society, groups crop up with some scheme or prophecy that shows that all biblical prophecies point to theirs as the last generation. So the Children of God may be strange, but they are not really that new.

The Children represent despair, doom, and destruction. They appeared like a meteor on the American horizon because they expressed something of the hopelessness of the times. They may hang on for years, appealing to those who like their dismal message of futility. But they have no real future in America.

The future belongs to those who know love, not hate; who wear a smile of Christian joy, not the scowl of bitterness; and above all, to those who know *hope* through Christ.

References

1. Danile St. Albin Greene, *The National Observer* (15 April, 1972),

p. 1.
2. Examples of immorality in COG, described in this section, come primarily from the Lefkowtiz Report, cited in the text.

For Further Reading

Drakeford, John D. *Children of Doom.* Nashville: Broadman Press, 1972.

Ellwood, Robert S., Jr. *One Way: The Jesus Movement and Its Meaning.* Englewood Cliffs, N.J.: Prentice-Hall, Inc., 1973.

Enroth, Ronald M., Ericson, Edward E., Jr., and Peters, C. Breckinridge. *The Jesus People: Old-Time Religion in the Age of Aquarius.* Grand Rapids: William B. Eerdmans Publishing Co., 1972.

4. Zen Buddhism

Looking Through the Third Eye

So you want to understand Zen Buddhism? Better you should forget it and have a cup of tea.

So say the best Zen Masters. Above all, don't ask one of them to explain Zen. He might smile and hand you a flower, having thereby exhausted the depths of the world's second-oldest religion. On the other hand, he might slap your face. One Master threw an inquirer into the mud to show that an experience of mud is better than hearing words about Zen. Any of these actions would be equally valid, and equally invalid, expressions of Zen Buddhism. But most likely the Master would merely ignore your question, for Zen can be neither explained nor understood. It can only be experienced.

Looking through the two eyes of intellect and emotion, the mind and the feelings, one can never see life as it really is. One may know a few fleeting things *about* life, but life itself eludes these eyes. Only by looking through what some Zen followers call "the third eye," the eye of intuition and enlightenment, can one penetrate life's mysteries and paradoxes. By means of the third eye of "satori," one moves from secondhand knowledge *about* life to the overwhelmingly wonderful firsthand experience of life itself.

At least, an American trying to summarize the basic motifs of Zen might put it that way. Probably a "Zennist," or Zen Buddhist, would not put it that way, or any other way. Since Zen is inexpressible, why try to express it? Like quicksilver, Zen always eludes our grasp. We may try to box it in with words and definitions, but it easily slips free of our explanations. Words are mere marks on paper or noises in the air, and they can no more capture the essence of Zen than a butterfly net can capture the breeze. Whatever statement one makes about Zen is bound to be false, including this one. The better and more accurate the explanation, the more it falls short of the true essence of Zen.

One Zen spokesman said, "Frankly, I don't know what American Zen is, and I don't think anybody else does." The greatest Zen Masters are those who know the least. A novice knows far more about Zen than an aged Master who has pondered Zen all his life. That explains why a Zen pupil could say, "I owe everything to my Master, for he taught me nothing."

But if you insist upon understanding, try this: "What is the sound of one hand clapping?" Or this: "Where was your face before you were born?" These are *koans*, Zen riddles or puzzles which are said to lead to enlightenment. If they stump you, ponder this poem:

> An old pond;
> A frog jumps in;
> The sound of water.

That little poem, or *haiku*, is said to contain the total meaning of Zen Buddhism. Countless people have overcome suffering, glimpsed their true inner nature, and have been marvelously liberated into the fullness of life just by understanding this little poem. Perhaps we should go back and read it again.

If this sounds like nonsense, you are making progress. Zen is indeed non-sense, or beyond sense in its ordinary or intellectual dimensions. It cannot be understood; in fact, Zen greatly discounts the value of *understanding* per se as being relatively useless anyway.

Zen Buddhism, whatever it is, is one of the oldest religions in the world, but one of the newest in America. It originated in ancient India, was modified in China, reached its greatest development in Japan, and has now achieved such a solid foothold in America that it looks like the beginning of an important new chapter in American religious history.

This chapter is an attempt to look through this "window to the East." It won't help you understand Zen, but it might give a few clues about what it is you are not understanding.

The Origin of Zen

Like Christianity, Buddhism is divided into a number of denominations, one of which is Zen. When Buddhism was about a thousand years old, Zen emerged as a reform movement, seeking to return to the purity of original Buddhism. In some ways, the Zen movement is comparable to the Protestant Reformation in Christian history. Seen another way, Zen may be called a synthesis of the religious insights of both India and China.

Buddhism had its birth about 525 B.C. in the foothills of the Himalayas, near the present border of India and Nepal. Siddhartha Gautama, a sensitive prince who had grown up in luxury, tried to plumb the meaning of life and suffering. One beautiful night in May he sat down under a fig tree in Gaya, India, and, pressing his palms to the ground, vowed never to move from that spot until he gained insight into the meaning of life, suffering, and death.

All night he sat in deep meditation. He passed through several stages of awareness, and all of his previous lives became as open books to him. Suddenly, in a blinding flash of enlightenment, the universe became clear to him. That night Gautama became "an Enlightened one," thus a Buddha.

As the original Buddha shared these insights, disciples gathered around him, and a new religion was born. Not until about 150 years after his death were any of his teachings written down, to become the nucleus of Buddhist scriptures. The Buddhist world soon divided into two great traditions, similar to the Catholic-Protestant division in Christianity. Hinayana Buddhism prevailed in southern countries. It was strict, orthodox, and gave close attention to Buddhist scriptures. The more liberal Mahayana Buddhism spread in northern areas, especially China and Japan. It gave more emphasis to the spirit and enlightenment of Buddha and less to his scriptures and teachings.

Zen originated about A.D. 527 in an effort to reform the Japanese branch of Mahayana Buddhism. Zennists derived their inspiration from Buddha's well-known Flower Sermon. One day 2500 years ago his disciples asked for instructions. The Great Buddha said nothing. Instead, he simply held up a golden lotus. A man named Bodhidharma carried the insight of the silent lotus into China and became the father of Zen.

Bodhidharma felt that disputing various Buddhist texts and doctrines completely missed the *message* of Buddhism, namely enlightenment. He withdrew to meditate in complete silence for nine years. He refused to see those who came to him for instruction until one young man cut off his arm and sent it in as a token of his seriousness. Bodhidharma taught this young man and others to deemphasize the *writings* of Buddha and to seek instead his *experience* of enlightenment. Thus Zen Buddhism was born. The word "Zen" comes from the Chinese "Ch'an," which in turn comes from a Sanskrit word meaning meditation or insight gained by meditation.

Zen has only lately come to America, but it is making itself right at home. It was believed by some Japanese-Americans in California, but since the 1950s has won numerous converts from the general population. Some think the growth of hippies, the drug culture, and the dropout alienation of American youth was influenced by Zen Buddhism, served up with espresso coffee during the "Beatnik Generation."

Expressing the Inexpressible

Zen is not a verbal religion. It has no preachers, for there is nothing to preach. It is called "the wordless sect," for it avoids scriptures, doctrines, and creeds. True Zen cannot be expressed, explained, or even communicated. It can only be experienced personally here and now.

To a Western mind, Zen may appear irrational, even foolish. According to Alan Watts, "Zen does not attempt to be intelligible, that is to say, capable of being understood by the intellect. The method of Zen is to baffle, excite, puzzle and exhaust the intellect until it is realized that intellection is only thinking *about;* it will provoke, irritate and again exhaust the emotions until it is realized that emotion is only feeling about, and then it contrives, when the disciple has been brought to an intellectual and emotional impasse, to bridge the gap between second-hand, conceptual contact with reality, and first-hand experience!" [1]

Some Masters flatly refuse to speak of Zen at all, either because they know nothing to say or feel that words are useless. One Master, asked by his pupil why he would not speak of Zen, replied, "Because it turns my stomach." They feel that "He who knows does not speak; he who speaks does not know."

Perhaps no modern religion puts such a premium upon *silence* as does Zen. That could be one part of its appeal in this media-saturated culture. Zennists meditate in silence, take their meals in silence, and perform their work in silence; and many masters instruct their pupils in silence. They are as careful not to waste words as they are not to waste food. Even lay visitors to Zen retreats are cautioned to speak as little as possible, and "idle chatter" is absolutely forbidden.

The value of silence is caught in some widely quoted Buddhist verses which say:

> When they curiously question thee,
>   seeking to know what It is,
> Do not affirm anything, and do not deny anything.
> For whatsoever is affirmed is not true,
> And whatsoever is denied is not true
> ....
> Therefore, to their questionings
>   offer them silence only,
> Silence—and a finger pointing the Way? [2]

Zen is an effort to go beyond rationality to non-sense, beyond man's "monkey mind" that keeps jumping around. When asked what enlightenment is, a Master may reply, "Three pounds of flax" or "A stump to tie your donkey to." If a pupil asks, "What shall I do if I have nothing?" the Master may reply, "Throw it away." Zen purposely forces reason to wrestle with absurdity, contrives to overwhelm reason and throw it against the wall "with the desperation of a cornered rat."

Zennists probably do well to avoid words, for the few words they use make little or no sense. One of their favorite chants to awaken Buddha-consciousness, comparable perhaps to the Christian Doxology, repeats over and over:

> Form is not different from emptiness;
> Emptiness is not different from form.
> Form is precisely emptiness;
> Emptiness is precisely form.[3]

Three Key Words

Despite their disdain for words, there are three words which at least point to, if they do not capture, some of the meaning of Zen. They are *koan*, *zazen*, and *satori*. The goal of Zen is satori, which is achieved through the koan and zazen.

A koan is a riddle or puzzle, a sort of mental dilemma without a rational answer. There are at least seventeen hundred Zen koans, such as:

> What is the sound of one hand clapping?
> When the Many are reduced to One, to what is the One
>   to be reduced?

That may sound like "How high is up," but Zen koans have a purpose. It is only by working through these koans that one reaches satori, enlightenment. Life itself is a giant koan, and realizing this helps one accept the world as it is without trying to change it. There are common koans that all Zen pupils must work through, and Masters may assign specific koans which they feel are particularly appropriate for individual pupils.

One interesting koan says, "Imagine you are hanging from a tall tree. You are not holding on to the tree with hands or feet, but only by a branch clenched in your mouth. An inquirer comes along and asks the meaning of Zen. What would you say?"

The koan has been compared to conviction in Christian terminology. Just as a person cannot be converted until he is under conviction—that is, confronts and admits his lostness—so a Zennist cannot be enlightened until he confronts his koans and admits the utter impossibility of understanding life by rational or intellectual means.

The second key word is *zazen,* which means to sit in meditation. To "sit zazen" is a common Zen expression. It is not just vacant-minded idling, but sitting with a purpose to clear the mind and make room for the satori breakthrough.

Whatever Zennists believe or don't believe, zazen is their major *practice.* One may not be able to say what Zen is, but one can definitely say what Zen followers do: they sit. Perhaps the primary picture Americans have of Zen is of a turbaned figure, sitting cross-legged in the lotus position. Although there is more to Zen than zazen, without zazen there would be no Zen.

Zen Masters may crack your skull for asking about beliefs, but they give careful and precise instructions about how to sit zazen. One should use a small cushion, sit cross-legged, sway back and forth a couple of times until he feels like an oak rooted in the ground, and then sit perfectly still. The ears should be in line with shoulders and the nose in line with the navel; and above all, the back should be perfectly straight. The sitter should fix his eyes on the floor about three feet away and clear his mind of all extraneous thoughts. Sometimes a straight-backed chair may be used instead of sitting on the floor, a small concession to American custom.

Though one may sit alone, it is better to sit with a group in the *zendo,* meditation hall. A monitor may walk slowly up and down the rows of meditating Zennists, striking sharply with a long stick anyone who is dozing or whose back is not straight. A person who feels drowsy or in need of discipline may request such a blow by a slight nod of the head.

Many benefits are claimed for zazen. Its practitioners say it improves both physical and mental health. Sitting zazen can, its advocates say, give the body new vitality to throw off disease, balance the temperament to eliminate short temper and melancholy, improve work efficiency, reduce the number of accidents, and make the person more creative. It may also bring the highest merit of all, which is no merit at all. Doctors have discovered that in deep zazen, breathing and metabolism rates are greatly reduced, leading some to compare zazen with hibernation in animals. Some call it "sitting death."

The purpose of zazen is not health, but that mysterious breakthrough to satori. Sitting is by far the most rigorous discipline of Zen, especially for activistic Westerners. It quickly sifts out the serious from the casual students.

Satori, like all of Zen, is impossible to define. It is like a brilliant flash of intuition, insight, enlightenment—the Eureka of the inner being. It is a mental-spiritual breakthrough to a new level of knowing, a new dimension of reality. Those who have experienced it speak of the incredible joy, the peace of mind regardless of outward circumstances, and the love for fellow creatures that accompanies this experience. Some have compared satori to Christian conversion or being filled with the Holy Spirit. Wonderful as it is, satori may fade and have to be repeated. A remembered satori is of no value whatever, for Zen emphasizes only the *now*, the immediate experience.

Buddhism originated in satori when Gautama received enlightenment under the fig tree. Contemporary accounts say the hair on his chest curled to the left, but after the transforming satori the hair curled to the right. This was symbolic of the transformation of his entire life. Zen today does not promise that satori will curl your hair, but does promise total life transformation.

Though satori is the ultimate goal of Zen, it must not be sought. To seek satori would make it recede, for seeking would imply desire or dissatisfaction with one's present state. Desire for anything, even enlightenment, will prevent enlightenment. One receives satori when one has so cleared the mind as to reach that delicate balance between wanting and not wanting. Nor does one *achieve* satori; it either comes or does not come.

People who have experienced satori express it in different ways. One said that in satori, "One's body and mind will naturally fall away, and one's 'Original Face' [true self] will appear." The new insight is total, with complete awareness of self, others, and the universe. A woman named Chiyono, upon reaching satori, put it this way: "Passing through the bottom of the bucket that Chiyono has received, water does not accumulate; nor does the moon take shelter." Satori invariably brings a sense of calm and perfect confidence. By this experience the devotee becomes a Buddha or reaches Buddhahood.

Some physicians suggest that prolonged cutting off of blood circulation caused by sitting cross-legged may account for the lightness of brain and temporary "high" called satori. This may or may not be true in some cases, but to a Zennist it is irrelevant. What he values is the experience. How it is induced, whether by puzzling out a koan, sitting zazen, or restricting blood flow to the brain, makes little difference.

Is Zen a Religion?

Does a chapter on Zen belong in this book? Zen definitely is strange to a Westerner; it is new in this country; and, depending upon one's definition, Zen Buddhism does qualify as a religion.

Zen has no God to worship, no sacraments or ceremonies, no heaven to anticipate, no hell to dread, no doctrines to believe, no moral commandments to observe, no sabbath to keep. Above all, in Zen there is no "soul" to be concerned about. Although there is evil, there is no sin in a Christian sense of personal responsibility for wrongdoing. There is therefore no repentance, no salvation, and no faith in the Christian sense.

Buddha is revered, but not worshiped. A Zennist may use his stone Buddha image to crack nuts, so no idolatry is involved. Buddhism, including Zen, is both atheistic and pantheistic, but not theistic. That is, adherents could say without difficulty that God is nothing or that God is all, but never that God is a *person*. However, most Zennists get along well with Christians, Hindus, Moslems, and even atheists, for Zennists accept all religions and believe none of them, including their own.

The "Four Sublime Truths" of Buddhism (and Zen) are: Pain is universal; pain is caused by desire; pain vanishes when desire vanishes; and desire can be overcome through the eightfold path. The eightfold path includes (1) Right knowledge; (2) Right aspiration; (3) Right speech; (4) Right behavior; (5) Right livelihood; (6) Right effort; (7) Right mindfulness; and (8) Right meditation.

Zen starts where traditional Buddhism concludes, with the eighth step. After all, *Zen* means meditation, and some Zennists do not even bother with the first seven steps.

Satori leads to Nirvana, a psychological state of mind in which perfect equilibrium prevails. There is no desire, no anxiety, no uncertainty. All is in perfect balance, and all barriers fall away so that the mind is undifferentiated from horizonless infinity. The self is finally at one with the universe. Nirvana has been compared to the Christian concept of heaven, but there is really no basis for comparison.

One of the fundamental points of Zen psychology is *anatman*, literally, "no self." There is no individual in the sense of a separate and enduring person and therefore no soul. What we call a person is really a collection of particles and karmic forces in a temporary compound. These come together in a *skandha*, bundle, which holds together for a lifetime, then disperses again. The original Buddha's last words were, "All aggregates are transitory," meaning that every compound, including the human, is unstable and will eventually come apart.

Despite lack of a self, Zennists believe in reincarnation. What is to reincarnate? They hold to a "kinetic view of reincarnation," in which the karmic waves continue to ripple after the stone which made them has sunk to the bottom. These karmic waves will continue to move until they are put together in another *skandha* or bundle of particles. Essentially this is reincarnation of life energy rather than of a person. This of course rules out personal immortality or life beyond the grave in any meaningful sense. The ultimate goal is to reach such a state of enlightenment that karmic forces are stilled and the weary cycle of reincarnation is ended.

Buddhists have a vast collection of scriptures, or *Sutras*, but Zen largely ignores them. In fact, the Zen reformation originated in the contention that Buddhism had "petrified the flow of truth in the written word of scriptures." Zen followers do make limited use of *The Sutra of 42 Sections,* the *Lankavatara Sutra,* and the *Diamond Sutra.* However, they do not regard these as in any sense inspired or authoritative, for Zennists recognize no religious authority except experience.

Westerners often accuse Zen of a lack of morality. It is true that they have no rules, no commandments, no moral code. Some American "Beatnik Zen" students seized upon moral freedom to justify their own libertine lives, but this is a corruption of Zen. One Zen Master, asked about ethics, said, "Get Enlightenment; the rest follows." From Zen comes a willingness to let things happen as they will, a diminishing desire to control or change the universe. Therefore, large social programs of welfare, education, or ministry to those in need would not be a priority in Zen. They seek to "put inaction in action," for nonaction is always better than action. To let the earth alone and neither exploit nor rearrange it is probably the key to Zen's compatibility with ecology.

Zen in America

American Zen is growing, showing its usual adaptability. Of course, it has absorbed some American features, just as Christianity in Japan has taken on some Oriental flavor. American Zen is well organized and has even begun to evangelize. Perhaps as many as two thousand committed Zennists study at about twelve major Zen centers in this country. However, the influence of Zen in American life is far greater than that number might suggest.

In 1906 Soyen Shaku visited this country, preaching on Zen to interested audiences. His sermons were published and widely circulated. The Buddhist Society of America was formed in 1930 by Shigetsu Sasaki and was renamed after World War II as the First Zen Institute of America. Beginning in 1927, the world-renowned Zen scholar Dr. Daisetz T. Suzuki published numerous books in English on Zen. His Zen lectures at Columbia University in the early 1950s stimulated widespread academic interest. Zen was seized upon by the Beatnik Generation in the 1950s as an alternate reality to replace their rejection of America. One of these, Alan Watts, is sometimes called the Norman Vincent Peale of American Zen, for he more than anyone else popularized the movement in this country. His book, *The Spirit of Zen*, first published in 1958, is still considered a classic American introduction. However, it is probably too much to claim that hippies are the spiritual grandchildren of Zen.

By the late 1950s Zen was moving out of the coffeehouses into Zen Centers. Of the twelve or so such centers in this country, by far the most important is the Tassajara Mountain Center south of San Francisco. Located in rugged mountain country near Big Sur and Carmel, Tassajara has been called "the center of gravity" for Zen in America and indeed throughout the entire Western world. Situated on about five hundred acres of land, it has extensive facilities including a zendo, a monastery, and land for gardens and livestock. It also has facilities for weekend or week-long lay retreats (*sesskins*). Other major centers are in Shasta, California, New York City, and Boulder, Colorado.

Tassajara includes a monastery where interested students may come to study with a "Roshi," Zen Master. They may stay a few weeks or a few years; but eventually they must return to the world, for Zen does not withdraw but lives in the world. The practice of Zen has no relation to *place*, they are taught, and one can practice Zen just as well in secular employment as in a monastery. However, while one is in the monastery, training and discipline are strict.

Most who come to Tassajara are single, but there is provision for married couples. Women as well as men may rise to leadership and become "Roshi." There is almost a fanatic insistence of keeping the monastery clean, giving rise to the proverb "clean as a Zen monastery."

The daily routine begins at about 3:40 A.M., when a gong signals the time to rise. All are expected to be dressed and ready for meditation by 4 A.M. Meditation, with occasional exercise breaks, may last until about 6 o'clock. After breakfast and tea is clean-up time, followed by a work period. There is also time for study or an occasional lecture. The evening zazen is usually longer, and by 9:00 or 9:30 all are in bed. Like many of the newer cults in America, Zen places little emphasis upon sleep, affirming that the closer one comes to spiritual enlightenment the less sleep he will need. Some Zen Masters claim to take only two to three hours of sleep a day, most of that while sitting zazen. This rigorous schedule is generously adapted, however, for American lay visitors.

Taking food is probably the nearest thing to a religious ceremony in a Zen center. Followers are vegetarian, and the food is simple but adequate. The monks file into the dining room in silence and bow to both the left and the right before taking their seat. Such a silent bow was said by one woman to bring people closer together than lying in bed kissing. Before the meal each monk places his hands together in a spirit of thankfulness and meditates briefly on the origin of food—the part played by planter, harvester, and transporter in bringing it to his table—remembering the importance of rain, sunshine, and the good earth. He then asks, "Am I worthy to be the beneficiary of such marvelous gifts?" The meal itself proceeds in silence, though there may at the beginning be a repetition of brief selections from some suitable Sutra.

After the meal each washes his own bowl, a duty considered more sacred than prayer. There is absolutely no waste, though a few crumbs of food may be set aside as an offering for the poor. Later, these are placed outside for the birds.

Manual labor is a basic part of Zen. Work is respected; and everyone, even the highest Master, is expected to participate. There is no hierarchy of tasks, with humble KP considered as honorable as bookkeeping. From ancient times, Zen monks had a saying: "He who does not work for a day, neither shall he eat for a day." The pupils of one aged Master, who continued to work despite his frailty, out of pity hid his hoe. They had to give it back when the old man stopped eating. Most Zen centers have extensive gardens, and rural centers keep livestock to provide their own milk and cheese. At Tassajara, the goat pen is known as the "Goat Hilton." Each center is governed democratically, and most are self-supporting. They receive income from publications, the sale of various items, and guest fees. They do not beg, but will receive donations.

One feature of American Zen Centers is their provision for guests. Many are run somewhat like a health resort, including steep prices for weekend or week-long sesskins. One need not be a Zen convert to attend such a retreat. For example, the Shasta Center advertised a "Lay Training Program" for the summer of 1976. Their descriptions of what to bring, when to arrive, and planned activities could, with minor changes, have come from Glorieta or Ridgecrest Baptist Conference Centers. Among the rules for the week were total abstinence from smoking, drugs, liquor, chewing gum, and cosmetics. Modest clothing was required, and there was to be no reading, television, or radio. Above all, guests were cautioned against talking—it was to be a week of silence. Each person was asked to bring his own sleeping bag, "work clothes, . . . and loose pants or a wide skirt for meditation."

There is no pressure for those who attend such retreats to become Zen Buddhists. In fact, Zen more than any major world religion seems indifferent whether people join or not. Nor must one necessarily embrace Buddhism to adopt Zen. Some have attempted, with whatever success, to practice the art of zazen or meditation without accepting Buddhist concepts or world view. However, for those who desire it, these retreats may culminate in *jukai,* a sort of lay ordination comparable to Christian confirmation or Jewish Bar Mitzvah.

Unlike Hare Krishna, Zen devotees need not withdraw from the world. They may return, in fact are encouraged to return, to family, secular job, and ordinary activities in PTA—sometimes even in church. They can sit zazen at home, in a chair at the office, or even in their cars while stopped at a traffic light.

The Appeal of Zen

What makes Zen look so attractive to some Americans? For some it appears as a religionless religion, a welcome relief from personal guilt, sin, endless doctrines, commandments, and ancient Scriptures hard to understand. It puts man at one with nature, which some regard as the ultimate answer to problems in ecology. It has become increasingly popular in some quarters to blame Christianity, with its "subdue the earth" doctrine, for ecological problems.

The utter irrationality of Zen puts off some people, but has a strange fascination for others. Life itself seems like a giant koan, an insoluble riddle that rational intellect cannot penetrate. Zen relieves people of trying to make sense out of life. It is easier to accept the world than to try to understand it, much less change anything.

Drugs have played a large role in the growth of Zen in America, despite the fact that Zen discourages their use. The vast majority (some estimate 99 percent) of American Zen converts have been on drugs. For many the LSD high first introduced them to the possibility of extraordinary experiences on a new level or dimension. By LSD they achieved new insights, new awareness, new release. Perhaps many of them seek the same thing in satori without the harmful side effects.

Can there be a Christian Zen? Some people think so. After all, Christianity also has an ancient tradition of meditation and spiritual awareness. After centuries in the activistic West, perhaps Christians need to recover the practice of sitting in quiet meditation on God and self. Christian Zen, maybe. Christian Zen *Buddhism*, no way, for Christianity and Buddhism are flatly contradictory.

Zen Buddhism has no room for God, no room for the Bible, and no room for salvation. Most of all, it has no room for Jesus Christ as the Son of God. Therefore, it has no room for me.

References

1. Alan Watts, *The Spirit of Zen* (New York: Grove Press, Inc., 1958), p. 19.
2. Ibid., pp. 21-22.
3. Ibid., pp. 29-30.

For Further Reading

Dumoulin, Heinrich. *A History of Zen Buddhism.* Translated by Paul Peachey. New York: McGraw-Hill Book Company, 1963.

Humphreys, Christmas. *Zen Buddhism.* London: William Heinemann Ltd., 1949.

Johnston, William. *Christian Zen.* New York: Harper and Row, 1971.

Watts, Alan W. *The Spirit of Zen.* New York: Grove Press, Inc., 1958.

5. Astrology

Control from Outer Space

Why do some people succeed in life, while others fail? Why are some people prosperous, so that everything they touch turns to money, while others who work just as hard go broke? Why do some marriages prove happy and satisfying, while others are miserable or end in divorce? Why are some people kind and good, while others are cruel and brutal? Why do some people enjoy sturdy health and live to old age, while others are sickly and die young? In short, why do things happen as they do? And more importantly, is there any way you can determine in advance, and possibly even control, the kind of life you will have?

From the dawn of history man has puzzled over these and similar questions. Various methods of finding the answers have been used and discarded. Ancient priests read the shape of chicken entrails to predict what would happen; modern men read computers for the same purpose. But nobody knows for sure what will happen or why. Some shrug and resign themselves to some vague influence called "fate." Others look to the providence of God and personal responsibility.

For answers to why things happen, millions now look neither to God nor man, but to the stars and other planets. "Born under a lucky star" is more than a figure of speech. For growing multitudes it expresses a philosophy of life in a system called astrology.

Almost overnight astrology has become big business. Over 1,250 newspapers carry the horoscope column daily, five times as many as carry the Billy Graham column. Countless books, magazines, and charts encourage people to study the stars to predict the future. There are over ten thousand full-time professional astrologers in this country, and possibly 175,000 more part-timers who cast horoscopes for hire.

Some estimate that up to forty million Americans dabble in astrology, more or less seriously. Probably most of these glance at their horoscope just for fun. For others the ancient zodiac system is serious business. They will not plan a trip, make an investment, or set a wedding date without consulting the sky to see if the planets are favorable. In this scientific age of space travel and computers, the ancient art of reading astral omens is making an amazing comeback.

What is a horoscope, and how do you read one? What is the zodiac, and why do astrologers say the moon is in the seventh house? Is there any conflict between astrology and the Christian faith? How can I witness to my friends who are into astrology? How did astrology develop, and how has it changed over the centuries? These and similar questions are answered in this chapter.

What Is Astrology?

Astrology comes from two words, *astro* (star) and *logos* (word), and means "words from the stars" or the message of the stars to us. The word is a misnomer, for astrology is more concerned about the influence of the sun, moon, and five other principal planets than the stars. The basic idea of astrology is that these planets have a determining influence upon human life. According to this ancient system, the position of the planets at the time a person is born will determine that person's character, personality, and ultimate destiny.

Original astrology was probably connected with animism, the idea that the world and planets are living beings. This "aliveness of nature" meant that the sun, moon, and major planets were gods (or controlled by gods) with distinct characteristics. The qualities of the planet-gods would rub off on those born under their influence. Thus, people born under the sign of Mercury would be quick and industrious; those born under Mars would be militant and warlike; and those born under Venus, the goddess of love, would be sensitive and romantic. Today most people do not believe the planets are deities, but the idea of their influence remains.

However, the system is much more complicated. To visualize the zodiac and "heavenly houses," put a piece of one-inch masking tape around a basketball and mark off twelve equal sections of the tape. Imagine that the earth is in the center of the basketball. A line down the middle of the tape is the elliptic, the plane of the earth's orbit and the sun's apparent annual path. The orbits of the moon and other five principal planets will not vary more than about 9 degrees on either side of this elliptic. This is known as the "zodiacal belt" and is the only part of the sky of interest to astrology.

Because certain major constellations of stars along this strip of sky seemed to resemble animals, or at least were named for animals, this strip was named zodiac, which means circle of animals. The twelve are the Ram, March 21-April 19 (Aries); the Bull, April 20-May 20 (Taurus); the Twins, May 21-June 20 (Gemini); the Crab, June 21-July 22 (Cancer); the Lion, July 23-August 22 (Leo); the Virgin, August 23-September 22 (Virgo); the Scales, September 23-October 22 (Libra); the Scorpion, October 23-November 21 (Scorpio); the Archer, November 22-December 21 (Sagittarius); the Goat, December 22-January 19 (Capricorn); the Waterman, January 20-February 18 (Aquarius); the Fishes, February 19-March 20 (Pisces). Of these, only Libra is not an animal.

Each section of the zodiac was called a "house" because it was the habitation of the planet-god who occupied that section of the sky. In some systems, each house also represents a different aspect of earthly life. For example, the first house determined personal appearance, the second finances, and so forth. Other systems assume that different signs rule different parts of the body. Therefore, the head is ruled by Aries, the face by Taurus, the breast by Cancer, the torso by Leo, the genital area by Scorpio, and the feet by Pisces.

You can find out the details of your fate by means of a personal horoscope. Your horoscope can be general, such as those printed in the newspaper, or an incredibly detailed calculation based on the exact time and place of your birth. Professional astrologers refer to newspaper horoscopes as "slop astrology" and consider them worthless. A personalized horoscope can cost from two to over one thousand dollars, depending upon how detailed it is and how famous the astrologer who plots it is. Most "good" horoscopes cost around twenty dollars.

Another feature of astrology concerns the "star ages." This is of great interest now because we are supposed to have just passed out of the old age of Pisces into the new age of Aquarius. Millions of Americans, especially young people, would recognize the song *Aquarius* from the hit musical *Hair*. Part of it goes:

> When the moon is in the seventh house,
> And Jupiter aligns with Mars:
> Then peace will guide the planets
> And love will steer the stars.
> This is the dawning of the Age of Aquarius.

According to astrology, the earth enters a new star age about every two thousand years. Though there is no agreement about the dating, most astrologers consider 4,000-2,000 B.C. the age of Taurus; 2,000 B.C. to the birth of Christ the Age of Aries; and from Christ to the present as the Age of Pisces. Next comes the Age of Aquarius, which began (some say) in the second act of *Hair*. Some say the new age began in 1906, 1945, 1968; others say it won't begin until about A.D. 2,000. Because of the distinctive alignment of planets and stars, the new watery age is supposed to be a time of peace, prosperity, and love.

Astrology: Old and New

Nobody knows when or where astrology first began. Its origins are lost in antiquity. However, we know that some form of astrology is as old as recorded history and probably dates from the time when the first man looked at the first sky. Some of the earliest human records deal with astrology, and some regard systematic stargazing as the first science. Astrology may also be the oldest known form of religion.

By 2,000 B.C. astrology was already dominant in philosophy, politics, and religion. There were as yet no zodiac and no individual horoscopes. Most prediction had to do only with kings and the fate of nations. Many archaeologists believe that the mysterious Stonehenge megaliths in England were part of an ancient astrological temple-observatory, dating to about 1800 B.C. The Babylonian and Chaldean ziggurats were certainly observatories. Most of the ziggurats were about 270 feet high, built on seven terraces (which stood for the seven major planets known to the ancients). Here priest-astrologers observed the heavens, interpreted the signs, and led in worship rites. Many believe the Tower of Babel (Gen. 11:1-9) was such a ziggurat.

The Babylonians further refined astrology and, by careful observation and precise records, reduced it to a semiscience. The Greeks later accepted astrology, which swept in with the conquests of Alexander the Great to replace their own worn-out Olympian gods. The zodiac is a product of Greek geometry, perfected probably about two centuries before Christ. The Greeks also democratized the horoscope and extended its use to ordinary citizens.

Claudius Ptolemy shaped astrology into the system we now know. He was born in Alexandria, Egypt, about A.D. 100. His famous book, *Tetrabiblos*, has been the main textbook of astrology to this day. According to Ptolemy, the earth is the center of the universe; and the sun, moon, and planets revolve around the earth, which is both stationary and flat. These views reigned unchallenged until the sixteenth century, when Copernicus suggested, and Galileo's telescope confirmed, a heliocentric solar system in which the earth as well as the other planets all revolve around the sun.

Christ was born into a world largely dominated by astrology. His own birth was heralded by a mysterious star and attended by astrologers (Matt. 2:1-10). As Christianity grew, it had to confront the rival claims of pagan astrology. Up to the fourth century perhaps the most serious rival Christianity had was an astrology-based religion called "Mithra."

This rivalry was settled, at least for then, when the Roman Empire adopted Christianity as its official religion late in the fourth century. However, certain features of Mithra remained. The Christian Lord's day retained its Mithraic name of Sunday. Christians continued to use a calendar whose seven days and twelve months were inherited from astrology. The great Christian festivals of Easter (spring equinox) and Christmas (winter solstice) carried over much of the cultural baggage from their earlier history in astrology.

Early Christian leaders were well acquainted with astrology, and with few exceptions they vigorously opposed it as contrary to Christ. Repeatedly they urged Christians to worship the Son rather than the sun. Justin Martyr (second century) declared in his Apology that astrology was "deluded" and imposed by false angels. A generation later, Tertullian condemned all astrology and even tried to persuade Christians to ignore the December festival (which later became Christmas) because of its associations with astrology.

Without doubt the most influential early Christian thinker was Augustine (354-430), whose teachings dominated the church for almost a thousand years. He experimented with astrology as a youth, but after his conversion he became its most bitter and effective foe. He condemned as a "pernicious superstition" the "opinion that, apart from the will of God, the stars determine what we shall do, or what good things we shall possess, or what evils we shall suffer." Augustine examined many of the objections to astrology which are still being discussed, such as the problems posed by twins who share the same horoscope but whose lives turn out differently. Augustine's primary objection was not scientific but moral and theological. To attribute what happens to the stars, he felt, was a denial of God's sovereignty. To make man's acts depend on the shape of the sky rather than on his own decisions completely undercuts personal moral freedom and responsibility for one's acts, Augustine insisted.[1]

Because all the heavy guns of church and state were leveled against the old system, astrology declined but did not die. It simply went underground, to emerge again in more favorable times. Those times came, surprisingly, with the advent of a new religion in the seventh century. The Mohammedan religion transformed the culture of Europe, bringing new concepts in mathematics, chemistry, architecture, and medicine. The Moslem scientists also revived astrology and its ancient philosophical base, Aristotle. By the high Middle Ages, astrology was flourishing again, with kings and even popes consulting charts and horoscopes. Thomas Aquinas, the great theologian of the Middle Ages, reversed Augustine and gave the Church's blessing to a modified astrology. He accepted the influence of stars and planets, but insisted they operated only under the power and will of God.

The Reformation leaders Martin Luther and John Calvin rejected astrology, which is still the primary position of Protestantism. Luther said of astrology, "I have no patience with such stuff . . . You should persuade me that astrology is a true science! I was a monk, and grieved my father; I caught the Pope by his hair, and he caught me by mine; I married a runaway nun, and begat children with her. Who saw that in the stars? Who foretold that? Astronomy is very good, astrology is humbug." [2]

Humbug or no, astrology continued to reign supreme until a Polish astronomer, Copernicus, dealt the system a body blow. He published *De Revolutionibus Orbium Coelestium*, which suggested a heliocentric (sun-centered) system. His theory was later confirmed by aid of Galileo's telescope. The Copernican system completely invalidates the teachings of Ptolemy, upon which modern astrology is based.

However, instead of rejecting astrology, many people rejected Copernicus. Efforts to understand the cosmos divided and went in separate directions. *Astrology* moved in the direction of the cultic and magical, while *astronomy* moved toward science and ultimately led to modern-day space travel. However, astrology proved more popular (and more profitable). Many scholars cast horoscopes, in which they did not believe, to make a living while pursuing their real interests in astronomy. This led Johann Kepler to say, "Astronomy is the wise mother and astrology is her whoring little daughter, selling herself to any and every client willing and able to pay so as to maintain her wise mother alive."

Once again astrology went into temporary eclipse. Its decline in the fourth century was due primarily to Christian opposition; its seventeenth-century demise was the result of the exciting new "Age of Enlightenment." As in earlier reverses, however, astrology went dormant, not dead.

Modern Revival of Astrology

Today astrology is raging like wildfire, in the midst of the most remarkable comeback in its five-thousand-year history. Man's earliest cosmic science, often discredited but never demolished, is ascending, to borrow one of its own terms.

Every day untold millions of dollars, francs, lire, and marks change hands for astrological materials and fees. The clients may be young girls looking for romance, politicians looking for election, or executives facing business decisions. They may also be serious scientists, for part of the resurgence of astrology is a renewed interest and openness on the part of scholars. Some are willing to take a new look at an old system.

Astrology in America

In the summer of 1976 the Oakland Athletics baseball manager hired a comely astrologer to help his team get more hits and hex the opposition into more strikeouts. It didn't work, for the A's missed the playoffs. However, this was not the first time such was tried. In the 1930s P. K. Wrigley, owner of the Chicago Cubs, hired an "evil eye" to sit behind home plate and cast a whammy on opposing batters.

Not just in sports, but in every area of life, astrology is growing. Courses in astrology and how to cast a horoscope are offered at hundreds of colleges and some high schools. At least one college in Los Angeles is devoted exclusively to the study of astrology. Astrology books and magazines circulate by the millions. Time Pattern Research Institute has programmed a computer to crank out a ten-thousand-word horoscope in two minutes, with thirty thousand regular monthly customers. Zodiatronics Telephone Service provides computer horoscopes on two thousand college campuses. Radio and television have astrology programs, such as the popular "What's My Sign" panel show. Modern seers like Jeanne Dixon and Edgar Cayce make some use of astrology, as do many of the new cultic religions such as Satanism and witchcraft.

Of course, astrology is not really new in America. Puritan preachers in colonial America interpreted comets and falling stars as divine messages, and since frontier times American farmers have been careful to plant their crops when "the signs" are right.

Modern astrology, however, is barely a century old in this country. In 1875 Madame Blavatsky and Colonel Olcott founded the Theosophical Society, whose disciples later branched out to found the Rosicrucian Order. Both of these esoteric religious cults were deep into astrology and helped popularize its practice in America.

Perhaps the first professional astrologer in this country was Evangeline Adams, who established an astrology studio in New York City in the 1920s. One of her clients was the millionaire financier J. P. Morgan, who paid her handsomely for monthly astrological forecasts to guide his various business ventures.

However, astrology did not really catch on until after World War II. Its greatest boom has been since the mid-1960s.

Does Astrology Work?

Any evaluation of astrology must come to grips with the simple question of whether or not the system works. It must have some success to have lasted all these centuries. Of course, any system of prediction is bound to be right sometimes. Ancient astrology was used to predict the sex of unborn babies. Remarkably, it was right about 50 percent of the time!

There can be no reasonable doubt that the sun and moon do significantly affect conditions on earth. Their influences on agriculture and tides are obvious examples. Some psychologists now believe that men as well as women have cycles of mood closely related to, and possibly influenced by, the moon cycle. The effect of sunspots, atmospheric rays, and climate upon human physical and psychological health is under study; and the jury is still out.

However, most experts agree that there is no *scientific* support for astrology's claim that the planets influence human personality, character, and ultimate fate. Astrology is based upon Ptolemaic cosmology, which is demonstrably false. It overlooks the role of heredity in making us what we are. The zodiac, which is basic to the system, is purely imaginary, since there is nothing in the sky that really corresponds to its categories.

Moreover, astrology faces many practical problems that make it hard to take the system seriously. The old problem of twins who share an identical horoscope but live completely different lives seem fatal today, as it did centuries ago. There is also the problem of mass tragedies, such as an earthquake or airplane crash, when people with completely different horoscopes share a common fate.

In this age of supersonic jets, it is possible for a person to be born at *different times and places*. Consider a woman giving birth on a jet speeding nearly two thousand miles per hour, near the international date line. It would be possible for the baby to be "born" on different days, thousands of miles apart! He could have literally hundreds of horoscopes, all equally valid (or invalid).

However, absence of scientific support for astrology does not imply lack of other kinds of support. Indeed, for some people astrology *does* seem to work. Much of it is merely a good general counsel, such as "Take extra care today" or "Be attentive to friends today"—good advice on any day. Many psychologists think horoscopic advice is largely self-fulfilling. If you *think* you are going to have a good day, chances are you will. Whether this result is caused by the planets or your mental outlook, the fact remains that you had a good day.

Many astrological predictions are vague and general. For example, on the day these words are being written, my horoscope reads, "More work arrives than you're set to handle." There is considerable truth in that for me, but the same would be equally true for most other days as well. I cannot see how it applies to my little three-year-old neighbor, who shares the same birthday.

An American astrology magazine for November, 1963, carried a prediction that many later seized upon as an amazingly accurate prediction of the assassination of President Kennedy. It read, "Apart from its direct link to things military, the powerful Mars influence incites much social unrest of the sort that erupts blindly into retaliative violence." By making their predictions so general as to cover *whatever may happen*, astrologers improve their success rate. Certainly social unrest can lead to violence, but it seems irresponsible to attribute the cause to Mars and do nothing to correct the human conditions that lead to such unrest.

Astrology in the Bible.—Since astrology is older than the Bible, the biblical writers were familiar with it. The Bible speaks often of astrology, especially in the Old Testament, always with a warning about its dangers. The Bible clearly and repeatedly condemns the practice of astrology when substituted for worship of the true God.

We have already seen that the Tower of Babel was probably an astrological observatory (Gen. 11:1-9). In the Israelite reforms, young King Josiah "deposed the idolatrous priests whom the kings of Judah had ordained to burn incense in the high places at the cities of Judah and round about Jerusalem; those also who burned incense to Baal, to the sun, and the moon, and the constellations, and all the host of the heavens" (2 Kings 23:5). Obviously these were astrologers who were undermining the worship of the true God. The frequent Old Testament mention of the "high places" may also have been connected with astrology.

There are repeated biblical warnings against worship of the sun, moon, and stars. Probably the frequency of these warnings shows that this was a serious and widespread problem at the time. The Bible says, "Beware lest you lift up your eyes to heaven, and when you see the sun and the moon and the stars, all the host of heaven, you be drawn away and worship them and serve them" (Deut. 4:19).

Other Bible passages which may have something to do with astrology include Genesis 37:9-11; Job 38:31-32; Daniel 2:1-28;

and Judges 5:20-21. The latter is one of few places where astrology is mentioned in the Bible without specific condemnation.

Of course, the major New Testament passage related to astrology is the story of the star of Bethlehem at the birth of Christ (Matt. 2:1-10). Much ink has been spilled over this passage, but still no one knows for sure what it means. Some have suggested it was a comet, a meteor, or a nova (new star). Some astronomers say that early in 6 B.C. there was a rare conjunction of three planets, Mars, Jupiter, and Saturn, and the magi may have seen it as a fulfillment of the prophecy that "a star shall come forth out of Jacob" (Num. 24:17). At any rate, it appears the star of Bethlehem was a miraculous event, provided for that occasion, and not a prediction from ordinary astrology.

A Christian and astrology.—Can a Christian believe in astrology without compromising his faith? Millions of Christians do read their horoscopes, but probably most do not take it too seriously. Astrology can be an interesting hobby, but if one takes it seriously it can lead to rejection of God and his providence.

The most serious religious objection to astrology is that it denies moral freedom and responsibility. If your deeds are determined by the stars, then you are not responsible. Your sins are not your fault; you couldn't help it; the stars are to blame. This can lead to escapism.

Astrology can also lead to fatalism, a helpless resignation to events over which you have no control. If you believe your future is already determined by the stars, there is little incentive for you to try to determine your own future.

Most Christians, if they think about it, would feel uncomfortable with a practice so clearly forbidden in the Bible. As fun and games, perhaps astrology is harmless. Taken seriously, it is idolatry.

What Astrology Says to Us

The tremendous interest in astrology tells us much about ourselves. Whether true or false, the system tells us more about the stargazers than the stars.

Many people feel an overwhelming need to know the future.

Not content with today, they seem desperate to look ahead to tomorrow. This curiosity about the future seems common to all humanity and is as old as mankind. In moderation there is nothing wrong with this. However, taken to extremes, this indicates insecurity, fear, and lack of faith in God. Jesus urged his disciples to live responsibly now rather than engaging in idle speculations about the future (Acts 1:8).

Predicting the future, "divination," is one of man's oldest activities. Across the centuries many methods evolved for forecasting the future. Ancients tossed the entrails of a freshly killed chicken on the ground and from their shape predicted coming events. Others preferred to read the future in the liver of freshly killed animals or the flight of birds or the way leaves swirl as they fall.

Still other cultures' intent to know the future evolved Tarot Cards, I Ching, witchcraft, and "seers" like the modern-day Jeanne Dixon and Edgar Cayce. All of these systems work to some extent. A well-informed person today can consult chicken entrails, a crystal ball, Tarot Cards, I Ching—or the horoscope—and have at least a general idea of some things that may happen in the future. He can do the same without consulting any of them.

The sudden popularity of astrology indicates the low esteem in which modern science and technology are held. Some observers think astrology is popular precisely *because* it is irrational and unscientific. Three centuries of modern science in the West promised far more than it has delivered. Rigid scientism has taken away mystery, wonder, and transcendence. We know more about the material world, but less about ourselves. We have more material goods, but the quality of life seems lacking. Technology has added years to our life, but has not given meaning to those years. In crowded and polluted cities, life can be lonely, impersonal, empty. Man feels out of touch with the universe as well as with his local community.

In such a time, people are open to mystical and cultic movements. Astrology attempts to bring the individual back in touch with his environment. It is not just that astrology is more respectable these days; traditional science is *less* respectable.

Another reason for the rise of astrology is the failure of traditional religions to satisfy people's spiritual needs. Many people feel alienated from their churches. They feel the churches have become cold and lifeless, with no sure word about the ultimate meaning of life. Most members of the new religious cults in America are former church members. A Christian with a personal relationship with Jesus Christ will feel no need for astrology or any of the other cults.

Conclusion

Astrology is the secular residue of what was once a great pantheistic religion. It is a giant game, a "cosmic Monopoly," played on an imaginary board called a zodiac. Originally it was polytheistic, worshiping many gods. Today most of the religious force has been drained off, leaving astrology as a secular movement which attributes events to fate, chance, or the planets. It has no real room for either gods or God.

No doubt many Christians will continue to dabble in astrology. Certainly it is no big deal if a Christian wants to read his horoscope. Problems begin, however, if he takes it seriously.

References

1. Saint Augustine, *The City of God,* Book V, chapters 1-8. Found in Philip Schaff, ed. *Nicene and Post-Nicene Fathers,* Vol. 2 (Grand Rapids: William B. Eerdmans, 1956), pp. 84-89.
2. James B. Jornstad and Shildes Johnson, *Stars, Signs, and Salvation in the Age of Aquarius* (Minneapolis, Minnesota: Dimension Books, 1971), p. 86.
3. William J. Petersen, "Astrology," *Those Curious New Cults* (New Canaan, Connecticut: Keats Publishing, Inc., 1975), p. 32.

For Further Reading

Cooper, John Charles. *Religion in the Age of Aquarius.* Philadelphia: The Westminster Press, 1971.

Jornstad, James B. and Johnson, Shildes. *Stars, Signs, and Salvation in the Age of Aquarius.* Minneapolis, Minnesota: Dimension Books, 1971.

McIntosh, Christopher. *The Astrologers and Their Creed.* New York: Frederick A. Praeger, Publishers, 1969.

[Zolar] King, Bruce. *The History of Astrology.* New York: Arco Publishing Co., Inc., 1972.

6. Transcendental Meditation

The McDonalds of the Consciousness Smorgasbord

Joe Namath, quarterback for the New York Jets, takes the snap and fades back to pass. Huge defensive linemen lunge toward him, but Joe ignores them. He calmly peers downfield, then coolly spirals the football to an open receiver for a touchdown. Then Joe turns to the camera and says, "Football is an incredibly chaotic situation on the field. A quarterback must be calm and relaxed out there. He needs mental clarity, concentration. TM helps me achieve it."

This clip is from a twenty-minute color film extolling the benefits of TM, especially for athletes. One major-league baseball player credits TM with raising his batting average almost 150 points, and over half of the Philadelphia Phillies are into TM. A corporate executive now has Wall Street pressures under control, thanks to TM, and a Presbyterian pastor with a history of heart trouble says that without TM he would be out of the ministry. TMers, as its practitioners are called, credit TM with giving them vigorous health, sparkling personalities, and inexhaustible energy.

What is this marvelous key that unlocks the universe, this magic formula that can tame the wild forces of life and allow us to become the persons we always wanted to be?

Transcendental Meditation, mercifully shortened to TM, is a system of quiet meditation combining modern psychology and ancient Hindu techniques. Sometimes called the "turn-on of the seventies," TM is a franchised American offering of perhaps the world's oldest method of human renewal, sitting quietly with the mind at rest.

But TM is more. Its advocates say there is now scientific proof that by use of its secret *mantra* harried moderns can achieve a fourth dimension of consciousness, totally different from wakefulness, sleeping, or dreaming. This "transcendent state" of total awareness taps the "sources of thought" and brings incredible benefits in health, personality, and social relationships. Widespread use of TM will banish hunger, eradicate crime, and forever banish war, making human conflict merely an unpleasant memory of man's primitive state.

Practically unknown in this country even a decade ago, TM is now sweeping the country. It was introduced here by Maharishi Mahesh Yogi, an Indian holy man and Hindu monk. He moved quickly from a Himalayan cave to the world's center stage in 1967 when he reportedly converted the Beatles, among other show-business personalities. TM became an overnight sensation. From a paltry 225 TMers in 1965, America has perhaps 1,000,000 in 1977, with about 30,000 new converts per month. They include psychiatrists, priests, students, businessmen, housewives, college professors, cab drivers, federal prisoners, drug addicts in rehabilitation, radical youth, little old ladies, and children as young as four.

Nor is TM alone. The vast American market for introspection has drawn a number of suppliers, ranging from Esalen to Zen to Yoga to Est. Despite surface differences, most of them offer substantially the same opportunities to plumb the depths of one's inner being in self-reflection.

After an era dominated by rationalism and efforts to harness the material world, neither of which have been fully satisfying, modern Americans have in recent years launched an intense investigation of the inner world of self. TM is leading the way in the biggest introspection binge in history, a "consciousness revolution." Astronauts may give way to "psychonauts" in our mad rush to explore and possibly conquer "inner space."

What Is TM?

TM can be incredibly simple or deceptively complex, depending on how you want it. At its simplest, it is merely the practice of sitting quietly for fifteen or twenty minutes twice a day while meditating peacefully on some pleasant-sounding word whose meaning is irrelevant. However, TM is also the subject of complex university and hospital studies involving some of the keenest minds in America, most of whom admit we have not yet scratched the surface of understanding the potential of TM and similar methods of self-understanding.

One TMer who went into the movement with considerable skepticism later concluded that "It is a profoundly simple method for relieving stress and simultaneously summing up dormant physical energy through deep rest. An ancient technique originated by the Vedas, one of India's oldest traditions, it results in a physiological state (the "transcendental state") which is distinctly different from the other three states of consciousness—sleeping, waking, and dreaming." [1]

The cumbersome term "Transcendental Meditation" puts some people off, raising visions of bearded gurus sitting on nail beds or coiled in boa constrictors. Some connect TM with Oriental fad religions, and indeed its religious connections are part of its current controversy. However, most TMers are quite ordinary folks, mostly middle class; and most of them have no plans to change their religious affiliations.

In TM one clears the mind of all thoughts except the secret *mantra*, assigned by the instructor. One may silently speak the mantra over and over, slowly, peacefully, until other thoughts recede and fade out of the mind. After awhile even the mantra begins to recede, and the TMer finds himself in a new dimension of total awareness.

Perhaps the basic assumption of TM is that there are other states of consciousness beyond rationality and that TM has blazed the trail to this wonderful new dimension. Such an idea is not new, even in America, for as early as 1902 William James said in his *Varieties of Religious Experience* that rational consciousness is but one type of awareness. Whether we recognize it or not, all around us are entirely different forms of consciousness which can be realized if we but find the right key to unlock their secret.

TM claims to have the secret to part these filmy screens. One popular image of how TM works involves a comparison with the ocean. Just as the ocean surface is turbulent with movement and waves, so the surface mind (the conscious mind) actively grapples with thoughts. But, like the ocean depths, the mind's depths are a vast, uncharted frontier. By probing below the surface to the silent depths of the mind where thoughts are formed, we can confront thought in its formative or "prenatal" stages and shape it properly, so that when it bubbles to the surface of the mind, it is a good thought that evokes a proper response.

Actually, TM is merely the technology of which the basic theory is called the Science of Creative Intelligence. In this country SCI has branched out like any conglomerate, under the umbrella of the World Plan Executive Council, with headquarters in Los Angeles. In addition to meditation, TM is also big business, with an annual income said to be nearly forty million dollars. They also own 465 acres in New York's Catskill Mountains, including a 350-room hotel and a sophisticated printing and broadcast plant. The cornerstone of the TM empire is Maharishi International University (MIU), with campuses in Fairfield, Iowa, and near Santa Barbara, California.

Ancient Practices Updated

TM is a newly registered trademark, but the practice of meditation is older than recorded history. Every major world religion, including Christianity, has emphasized its merits. At some time in their history Judaism, Mohammedanism, and Christianity, the major religions of the West, have used mantralike devices to facilitate meditation.

However, meditation is most at home in the East, where it has for centuries been a fundamental part of Hindu, Buddhist, and Taoist religions. Perhaps the most fundamental concept of Eastern religion is escape from the illusiory material world to the *real* world of the inner self via meditation.

This ancient practice enjoys a startling revival today, franchised as TM. The painless new form of meditation was founded by Maharishi Mahesh Yogi, who was born on the banks of the Ganges about 1918. He received a degree in physics in 1940 from the University of Allahabad, but forsook natural science to spend 1940-1953 studying with a mysterious Guru Dev, considered a god by his followers, who refer to him as "Vedanta Incarnate." Apparently Swami Dev developed the basics of TM and charged his pupil the Maharishi to popularize it worldwide.

Swami Dev's pupil spent two years in meditation in a Himalayan cave, standard field work for a Hindu monk, and then after some years of wandering the forests of India took the name of Maharishi, which in Sanskrit means Great Sage. The Maharishi is a short plump man, with long gray hair and a full beard. He looks every inch the Indian holy man, complete with flowing white robe, a string of beads, and thong sandals, always carrying a flower.

By the late 1960s the Maharishi decided to take the product to the consumers, trying first England and then the United States. For some strange reason he was not well received. He looked and sounded strange, and many people looked upon his fantastic claims as another variety of faith-healing. The Beatles soon wearied of meditation and publicly renounced their guru; Mia Farrow and other famous converts also dropped out. The Maharishi attempted a barnstorming tour of America, but one advance man complained, "He couldn't even draw flies."

But the shrewd little guru was far from finished. At his fifty-eight room ashram in Rishikesh, India, he gradually rebuilt his collapsed empire. Later he moved to Italy; then in 1971 he launched a New World Plan, to center in the United States. This time it caught on, and by 1972 *Time* magazine could report that "the guru has generated what may well be the fastest-growing cult in the West."

The Maharishi succeeded in his second effort for two reasons: America was different, and TM was different. In the mid-60s America was not yet caught up in the journey inward. Besides, the guru had no adequate plan to merchandise his technique, a failing he had remedied by 1970. Now he charged hefty fees; and what Americans would not have as a gift they rushed out to pay good money for. With Madison Avenue promotions foreign to its Ganges origin and a commercialism contradictory to its Hindu roots, TM hit the big time on the American self-discovery market.

Meditation for Moderns

How does TM work? The technique has been tailored some for the American market, ruling out painful cross-legged sitting and strange diets. The procedure is remarkably simple and easy, and virtually anyone can do it. All you need, said one TMer, is a mind and the ability to have a thought—which might, even so, eliminate some.

An interested person can go to the local TM center; most cities have them. Courteous, conservatively dressed attendants will talk with you, give out literature, and invite you back for free explanatory lectures. The Maharishi has laid out a seven-step program of induction which teachers call "The Seven Steps of Learning to Unfold the Full Value of Creative Intelligence." First, you attend a free lecture, about an hour and a half, giving some idea of the potential for personal growth. Second, another free lecture explains more fully the mechanics of the TM technique. If one is still interested, he signs up at this point and pays the fee for further instruction. The third step is a private interview with an accredited teacher of TM, in which you are formally initiated into the movement and are given your secret mantra. Steps 4 through 7 are small group meetings with other initiates, taken on four consecutive days, in which TM teachers and "checkers" (teachers' aides) give both group and individual instructions in the actual practice of meditation, with some trial runs.

That's it. Then you are on your own, but you can come back without extra charge for refresher studies. Some go on to further instruction, called "rounding," in which one meditates all day for several days at a time. However, few go this far, and it is not recommended for new meditators. Some evidence suggests that rounding can be severely damaging in some cases.

TM initiation costs $125 for adults, $65 for college students, $55 for high-schoolers, and $35 for middle-school students. A couple and their children under fifteen may all enroll under the family rate of two hundred dollars, and children from four to ten can get in for two weeks' allowance. Payment must be in full, in advance.

The initiation ceremony is the most cultish part of TM, and it puts some people off. Even committed TMers have urged its revision, partly because in the initiation as nowhere else, heavy Hindu religious overtones come through. The initiation is called *puja*, which means invocation or an act of worship. The initiate must bring three pieces of fruit, a new white handkerchief, and six long-stemmed cut flowers. All of these are symbolic. The flowers represent the flowers of life, the fruit the seed of life, and the handkerchief the cleansing of the spirit. No TMer may pass up the initiation; it is required.

The leader lights candles and incense, places the fruit, flowers, and handkerchief on an altar under a color portrait of Guru Dev, and then goes through several minutes of chants and prayers, making "an offering of thanks to Guru Dev for sharing his knowledge with us." The *puja* includes, among other things, these invocations:

> Offering the invocation to the lotus feet of
>> Shri Guru Dev, I bow down.
> Offering a seat to the lotus feet of
>> Shri Guru Dev, I bow down.
> Offering an ablution to the lotus feet of
>> Shri Guru Dev, I bow down.[2]

After the *puja*, the leader whispers into the ear of the initiate his *mantra*, a Sanskrit word of two or three syllables. The mantra is one of the most mysterious and secret parts of TM. Despite efforts to keep it secret, it is reliably reported that each TM teacher is verbally issued a kit of seventeen mantras directly from the Maharishi. Mostly they are names of Hindu deities, but are meaningless to most Americans. Since each teacher has the same seventeen, many share the same mantra. The mantra idea originated in the fourteenth century B.C., but they have never been written down and rarely spoken out loud. To *think* the mantra is refined, but to *say it aloud* makes it gross.

Most American TMers are not aware that their mantra is the name of a Hindu deity or that it is chosen at least partly for its vibrations. These vibrations, even the separate sounds of each syllable, have their own significance. They are said to evoke God-consciousness, whether one knows it or not. Just as a person who flips a light switch need not understand electricity, for the light comes on just the same, so a TMer need not know that he is evoking deities. God-consciousness results all the same when he mentally pronounces his mantra.

The initiate must sign an agreement "that I will not directly or indirectly impart or disclose to anyone the mantra I receive or its instructed use." One TMer explained that, "for reasons that are scientifically unexplainable, revelation of the mantra turns a process of relaxed simplicity into an area of strain and confusion." [3]

Leaders warn that failure to heed this warning can lead to headaches, nervousness, and nausea. The mantras are supposed to be chosen to fit the individual. One man said to his TM teacher, "Joe and I were talking and it turns out we have the same mantra, and we have nothing in common." "Yes, you do," replied the teacher. "You are both fools."

Critics, however, regard the mantra as a sales gimmick and point out that concentration on any single idea, such as Hail Mary or some portion of the Lord's Prayer, would work just the same. In fact, mantralike words were common in medieval Christian mysticism. A fourteenth-century Christian treatise, *The Cloud of Unknowing*, says, "Clasp this word tightly in your heart so that it never leaves no matter what may happen. This word shall be your shield and your spear."

Meditation is easy, and it would be hard to find a wrong way to do it. However, there are a few rules: never meditate immediately after eating, and never at bedtime. Those who have done the mantra bit at bedtime find themselves still wide awake at 4 A.M., for reasons not entirely clear since it is supposed to be relaxing. The ideal is to meditate twenty minutes before breakfast and twenty minutes before dinner. Leaders recommend that one not exceed these times, for just as too much sleep can make one drowsy, too much meditation becomes harmful.

Easy as it sounds, many drop out after a few weeks or months. One Massachusetts man said, "Look, I really tried, I paid my $125, attended all the sessions, and submitted to a ridiculous initiation ceremony. I meditated for six months, and do you know what happened? I fell asleep every time." [4]

Be Who You Want to Be

The benefits claimed for TM read like a testimonial for frontier snake oil. Excellent health, a sparkling personality, no crime, and a world without war—these are just a few of its claims. It would be hard to imagine any kind of human benefit that has not been claimed for TM. One TM brochure just cut through all the details and proclaimed TM as "the solution to all problems." [5] It boils down to this: By the use of TM you can reshape yourself into the person you really want to be, and you can reshape the world into the kind of place you want it to be.

Benefits to health are widely claimed and have been subjected to the most intensive investigation. The consistent practice of TM, it is alleged, can lower blood pressure, reduce the heart rate, reduce the amount of oxygen used, and significantly lower the risk of heart attack, stroke, ulcers, and respiratory diseases. In general, tests tend to confirm most of these results.

Psychological benefits are more difficult to validate. It is said that TM makes one more alert, more responsive, and more aware. It improves conversation, reduces depression, and improves sexual performance (except for Catholic priests; for some reason, the very same exercises help them forget about sex). It helps students with homework, and one mother even claimed that after TM her eighth grader cleaned up her room without being asked!

Through TM, its advocates claim, families are unified, the

generation gap bridged, athletes are motivated to excellence, and intrapersonal conflicts are avoided. Many speak of being more *aware*—one TMer was almost overcome by the beauty of a traffic light. The reds seem redder, the world fresher. "It's as if I had been looking at the world through smudged glasses that are now clean." A commuter claimed that TM gave him more maneuverability in traffic.

However, not all benefit equally. As many as thirty to fifty percent drop out after a few months, apparently not finding TM worthwhile. *Psychology Today* reported that "an extremely anxious person who has managed to restrain his anxiety may find that the deep calm of mantra meditation liberates nothing but his problems" and cites studies showing that some TMers develop ulcers, depression, and other problems.

Verification of TM claims has been difficult. Many of the tests have been conducted under TM auspices. Some physicians suspect a "placebo effect" in that people *expect* benefits and therefore tend to receive them.

Perhaps TM's most controversial claim is that it increases "creative intelligence." This reminds one of early Dianetics claim to raise IQ one point for each hour of "auditing." There is no evidence that TM has any substantial effect upon intelligence levels. The catchall claim that TM is the "solution to all problems" of course cannot be taken seriously.

In our nuclear age, war is one of our greatest crises; and TM claims to have its cure. The Maharishi teaches that war is just a cry of nature built up from the silent sighs of stressed individuals. If we bring peace to all individuals, then world peace becomes a reality.

No one knows for sure what the ultimate causes of war are. Perhaps personal stresses, especially of leaders, do play their part. However, it seems too simplistic to attribute all war to personal tensions and perpetual world peace to their relief. This theory ignores too many other factors.

It appears that TM definitely helps some people, slides off others, and apparently harms a few. In general, its benefits have probably been considerably oversold.

Is TM a Religion?

The single greatest fear the Maharishi and his leaders have is that TM will be defined as a religion. Why should a Hindu monk, who evolved a technique out of the Vedic scriptures and initiates people through invocation to Hindu deities, be so afraid of being labeled as starting a religion?

Presently TM is being taught in many public high schools and a few junior highs. Government grants paid for TM instructions for many public-school teachers, and facilities have been provided on campus for them to teach TM to students. TM is now taught on over three hundred college campuses, mostly at government expense. Tax money has funded a number of major TM projects, and Maharishi International University receives substantial tax support. If TM is defined as a religion, all this must stop.

There are lawsuits pending in a number of states to cut off public funding for TM on the ground that it is a religion. Of course, TM leaders are frantically fighting this. The Maharishi says flatly, "We are not a religion"; and the vice-president of MIU had a statement read into the Congressional Record that TM "requires no faith or belief whatsoever and is associated with no religion or philosophy." A TM public-relations spokesperson states that "Transcendental Meditation is not a religion or a philosophy and does not involve a code of ethics or a particular life-style. People of all faiths the world over practice TM twice a day and enjoy the benefits, finding no conflict with their religion." [6]

A Presbyterian pastor whose entire family became TMers said, "We have found no compromise in our commitment to Jesus Christ and to his church. Indeed, we have found that our entire life-style has become more Christian as we both give and receive love with less tension in our lives." [7]

Joseph M. Occio, a Catholic priest, writes that "the essentials of TM and SCI can validly coexist with Christianity. You can be a good Catholic and a practicing meditator."

However, many who have studied and experienced TM claim that it definitely is a religion. One writes, "TM is a very definite religion in a very definite disguise. Whatever the scientific benefits of TM, its religious functions become clear in the Maharishi's claim that 'Transcendental Meditation is a path to God.' " [8]

The Maharishi also said, "A very good form of prayer is this meditation which leads us in the field of the Creator, to the source of Creation, to the field of God." [9]

There is no doubt that TM originated out of religion, namely Hinduism. Its founder is a Hindu monk; its concepts are based on Hindu scriptures; and its world-view reflects that of its parent religion. *Psychology Today* reported that "the Science of Creative Intelligence, as it is called, is clearly the revival of ancient Indian Brahmanism and Hinduism. Its origins lie in the ancient texts— *Vedas, Upanishads, Bhagavad-Gita;* the teachings of the Buddha, and the synthesis of these traditions in Shankara." [10]

We have already seen that the *puja* includes invocation of Hindu deities. Religion comes through even more in the ceremony for training teachers of TM. Its invocation says, in part, "To Lord Narayana, to lotus-born Brahma, the Creator, to Vashishta, to Shakti, and to his son, Parashar, to Vyasa, to Shukadava . . . I bow down . . . At whose door the whole galaxy of gods pray for perfection day and night, adorned with immeasurable glory, preceptor of the whole world, having bowed down to him, we gain fulfillment." [11]

There seems no doubt that TM is indeed a religion. It certainly deals with religious questions. What is the nature of reality? What is the nature of man? What is the human dilemma, and how can it be solved? These are basic to TM, and they are religious questions by any standard.

However, it is also clear that for many of its members TM does not *function* as a religion. One meditator said he simply ignored the religious elements, which he termed "Hindu mumbo-jumbo," concentrating on the secular technique of meditation. Those who ignore the religious dimension of TM, including the vast majority of its American adherents, are therefore practicing an abbreviated version of TM. For others TM does function as a religion, even though they regard it as merely secular. It fulfills the need for prayer, worship, forgiveness, and even salvation through meditation, providing in effect a substitute for religion.

The Maharishi's denial that TM is a religion should be seen in context of Eastern thought. One characteristic of Eastern religions is precisely this: *to deny that they are religions.* Buddhism, the world's second-oldest religion, vigorously denies being a religion. The same is true of Zen, a form of Buddhism popular in America. Obviously, what is or is not a religion depends upon one's definition. The basic concepts, values, and world-view of TM mark it as a religion, though many of its practitioners may be unaware of that.

No doubt there are many sincere Christian TMers who have no intention of compromising their faith. At their deepest levels, however, the Maharishi and Jesus Christ cannot coexist. They represent fundamentally different views of the world, human nature, and the nature and cure of the human dilemma.

TM or Not TM

Anything that can get frantic Americans to *stop* for awhile can't be all bad. There are undeniable benefits to quiet meditation such as TM offers.

While one of the most popular, TM is by no means the only viable meditation technique. Some estimate there are as many as eight thousand ways to "turn on" in America, many involving meditation. The major medical response to TM is not that it does not work, but that *any* method of quiet meditation works just as well, and without the $125 fee. Dr. Herbert Benson of Harvard Medical School evolved a method that can be learned in one minute at no cost. It involves sitting comfortably, progressively relaxing every muscle from feet to face, breathing quietly, and mentally repeating the word "one" with each exhalation. "We're confident that our method of meditation—or any of half a dozen methods—would work as well," says Dr. Benson, whose book on the subject is called *The Relaxation Response.*

Some deplore the whole meditation movement as an unhealthy

escapism from the problems of real life. Many regard it as essentially irrational and socially irresponsible, a "new narcissism" that encourages the "deification of the isolated self." They say its sustained self-contemplation is a poor substitute for meaningful involvement in real life. It is true that TM lacks any significant social awareness, and its social ethics (as opposed to personal ethics) are almost nonexistent.

Other questions arise. If TM is so creative, why do its advocates often sound so trite and repetitious, like telephone recordings? If the mantra is really just a meaningless word, why the secrecy? Why do ministers and psychiatrists have difficulty joining? If TM really has the power to deal with human ills, what about the ethics of pricing it out of reach of the people who need it most?

If TM really can lead to physical health and material prosperity, why not give it a chance in India, where it originated, and where disease and starvation are so prevalent? One hesitates to conclude that it is because so few people in India can afford the $125 initiation fee. However, the history of religious exploitation makes it impossible to overlook this possibility.

Meditation is a positive good, and Christians probably should practice it more. There is no doubt that physical and emotional benefits could result from a regular time of relaxed meditation, or even a daily nap.

Christians have scriptural precedent for meditation. The New Testament says, "Finally, brethren, whatsoever things are true, whatsoever things are honest, whatsoever things are just, whatsoever things are pure, whatsoever things are lovely, whatsoever things are of good report; if there be any virtue, and if there be any praise, think on these things" (Phil. 4:8).

A Christian has every reason to take time to sit quietly and meditate. But there is no reason to embrace a Hindu system and pray to pagan gods while doing so.

References

1. Phyllis Battelle Van Horn, "How Transcendental Meditation Changed Our Family's Life," *Ladies Home Journal* (November,

1975), p. 162.
2. Robert B. Fulton, "Transcendental Meditation," *The Christian Century* (10 December, 1975), p. 1124.
3. Van Horn, p. 164.
4. Martin E. Marty, "Turning Out with TM," *The Christian Century* (29 October, 1975), p. 983.
5. Gary E. Schwartz, "TM Relaxes Some People and Makes Them Feel Better," *Psychology Today* (April, 1974), p. 44.
6. Letter dated July 16, 1976, from Cheryl Shadburne to Cecil White, Reference Librarian, Fleming Library, Southwestern Baptist Theological Seminary, Fort Worth, Texas. Available in Fleming Library Vertical Files.
7. John R. Dilley, "TM Comes to the Heartland of the Midwest," *The Christian Century* (10 December, 1975), p. 1131.
8. George E. LaMore, Jr., "The Secular Selling of a Religion," *The Christian Century* (10 December, 1975), p. 1135.
9. Ibid.
10. Colin Campbell, "Transcendence Is As American As Ralph Waldo Emerson," *Psychology Today* (April, 1974), p. 38.
11. "The TM Craze: Forty Minutes to Bliss," *Time* (13 October, 1975), p. 74.

For Further Reading

Bloomfield, Harold; Cain, Michael; Jaffe, Dennis. *TM: Discovering Inner Energy and Overcoming Stress.* New York: Delacorte Press, 1975.

Ellwood, Robert S. "The Maharishi Mahesh Yogi's Transcendental Meditation Movement," *Religious and Spiritual Groups in Modern America.* Englewood Cliffs, N.J.: Prentice-Hall, Inc., 1973.

Needleman, Jacob. "Transcendental Meditation," *The New Religions.* New York: Doubleday and Co., Inc., 1970.

Rowley, Peter. "Transcendental Meditation," *New Gods in America.* New York: David McKay Co., Inc., 1971.

7. Confronting the Forces of Evil

Satan, Demons, and Witches

Some say it began with the movie *Rosemary's Baby*, a 1968 box-office smash about the birth of a devil-child. Others point out that Anton S. LaVey, the "Black Pope," formed his Church of Satan in San Francisco as early as 1966. Certainly by the time William Blatty's *The Exorcist* hit the screen in 1973, the American rediscovery of devils and demons was well under way. Later movies like *The Omen, The Other,* and, more recently, *Look What's Happened to Rosemary's Baby* continued to appeal to a morbid fascination with dark occult forces in what some have called the American "Age of Evil."

This new emphasis upon evil surfaced at a desperate time in our history. Still shocked by the tragic death of a popular president, the nation was locked into a war in Vietnam that many regarded as evil. In a decade that some historians call "the desperate sixties," America was ravaged by a cultural revolution led by the young and resulting in a severely alienated subculture. Traditional values were shaken, and the home, industry, government, education, and the church were severely criticized and often rejected outright. In 1965 prominent churchmen proclaimed that even God is dead. If this tells us nothing about God, it tells volumes about the despair in our country.

The last decade has seen an unprecedented fascination with the occult. Devils, demons, and witches are making their greatest comeback since the Middle Ages. The occult's milder forms are seen in television programs like *Bewitched, Dark Shadows,* and the still-popular *Frankenstein*. Other programs, movies, and books express a more "hard core" portrayal of the demonic. Even the churches have in many cases revived the ancient practice of exorcism, or casting demons out of afflicted persons.

In *Rosemary's Baby* the closing scene shows the evil witch-leader Castavet crying in triumph:

> God is dead! God is dead and Satan lives!
> This year is One, the first year of our Lord!
> The year is One, God is done.

A year later LaVey, who played the role of Satan in the movie, wrote in his Satanic Bible that "Lucifer is risen, once more to proclaim: 'This is the age of Satan! Satan rules the Earth.' " [1]

The Devil has found new popularity in America. This chapter takes a look at our "ancient wretched foe" and cites some reasons for his new lease on life.

Satanism

On August 8, 1969, Charles Manson and his freaked-out "family" burst into the Los Angeles home of Roman Polanski, who had directed *Rosemary's Baby*. The Manson cult, dressed in Satanic black, slaughtered Polanski's wife, the lovely Sharon Tate, who was almost eight months pregnant. Several others were also killed and mutilated in a grisly Satanic ritual. When he was arrested later, Manson told newsmen, "I am Satan, and all my women are witches."

The Manson cult is only one of dozens, perhaps even hundreds, of Satanist cults in America. They range from the rather harmless Church of Satan, where middle-aged folks dance around an altar with a naked girl, to weird cults which practice animal mutilation and sacrifice, to the truly sinister and deadly cults of the Manson type.

Satanism may be one of the fastest-growing antireligions in America. The known Satan cults claim around fifteen thousand members, with many times that many sympathizers. However, most of the cults are secret, and there is no way to estimate their membership.

The First Church of Satan in San Francisco is the most familiar example of Satanism in America. Founded in 1966 by Anton Szandor LaVey, this "church" is dedicated to the principles of Satan, unrestricted practice of the seven deadly sins, and fulfillment of every selfish desire. The members have elaborate rituals for weddings, funerals, and child dedication to Satan. Even so, they are probably the mildest form of Satanism in America.

Born in 1930 in Chicago, LaVey was known as Howard Levy before he became the "Exarch of Hell" and founded the Satanist church. The "Black Pope of Satanism" is descended from Rumanian and Alsatian parents, including a gypsy grandmother who told him stories of vampires and witches in her native Transylvania.

As a teenager LaVey dropped out of school and joined the Clyde Beatty Circus as cage boy, watering and feeding the lions. He later rose to be assistant lion trainer. At age eighteen he left the circus and joined a traveling carnival, where he practiced magic and hypnosis and continued his experiments with the occult. A competent musician, LaVey also played the organ at a few tent revivals.

After his marriage, LaVey's wife urged him to settle down. He entered City College in San Francisco as a criminology major and later worked three years as a police photographer. In this job, he said, "I saw the grimiest side of human nature. People shot by nuts, knifed by friends, kids splattered in the gutter by hit-and-run drivers. It was disgusting and depressing." [2]

LaVey could not accept such events as "the will of God," as some Christians did; and he became convinced that the world was under the control of evil. After returning to nightclub work, LaVey began to invite a few friends to his home occasionally for the practice of occult arts. From this home "magic circle," LaVey decided in 1966 to launch his Church of Satanism. He shaved his head, put on a clerical collar, dressed in black, and topped off his new costume with a black headdress with pointed plastic horns.

Most Satanist meetings are held on Friday night. Members arrive after dark and are ushered into the "ritual chamber," which during the day serves as living room for LaVey and his attractive blonde wife Diane. The room is painted a "purgatory black," lighted only with a few black candles. The walls are adorned with Satanic symbols such as an upside-down cross and the upended star, which signifies a goat's head. There are various pentegrams on the floor and walls. For their rituals Satanists dress in black robes—the men with hoods, women without.

Satanist ritual centers around a couch on which a totally nude young woman reclines. Each week different women members volunteer to serve as the living "altar of flesh," a symbol of Mother Earth. Probably the real symbolism is sexual fulfillment, although at the LaVey church (unlike some others) Satanist worship does not necessarily culminate in public orgies.

One ritual popular with this cult is the Invocation of Lust, in which the Satanists may conjure up black-magic charms to help members win sexual conquests over people they want. Those who use such charms are encouraged to give their testimony at later meetings about its success.

The Invocation of Destruction is more sinister and has to be used carefully lest the group come afoul of the law. In rites similar to ancient voodoo, Satanists will sometimes cast a hex to harm those whom the leader or some member of the group want harmed. Some reports claim such a hex was cast upon the boyfriend of actress Jayne Mansfield shortly before both of them were killed in a car wreck.

Satanist beliefs are a hodgepodge of magic, rejection of Christianity, and exalting human indulgence. Perhaps the best summary of these beliefs is *The Satanic Bible*. This evil little book, dedicated to Marilyn Monroe and P. T. Barnum, has circulated more than 300,000 copies in America alone. Perhaps the heart of the Satanic Bible is the reversal of the seven deadly sins, all of which LaVey advocates. This book is built around nine major "Satanic statements," of which the first and central is "Satan represents indulgence instead of abstinence."

Of course, Satanism rejects Christianity outright. Satanists believe that God, if he exists at all, is a vague, impersonal force which they call the "balance of nature." He neither knows nor cares about humans. Christ they ridicule and mock as a "pitiful Galilean" whom they consider a fool and a failure. Some Satanist meetings display the cross upside down as a symbol of Christianity's dedication to death, whereas Satanism is dedicated to life.

Strangely, most modern Satanists do not believe in Satan as a real being. LaVey, who says his work is "raising the devil," says Satan is merely a symbol, the altar ego, or "a mirror image of that potential I perceive in myself." Every man is then his own Satan, and the Devil is no more real than God. To live for Satan means that man willfully controls his own destiny rather than knuckling under to the pressures of society.

Satanists believe that man is inherently selfish, sensual, and violent. Greed, lust, and hate are as natural to man as breathing, say the Satanists, and should be accepted and even celebrated. Man is merely an animal, sometimes better but more often worse than the four-footed kind. One reason Satanists sometimes use animal symbols or costumes in their rituals is to stress the "essential animality" of man.

LaVey stresses that the seven deadly sins have reversed proper morality. Every person, after a hard day's work, should commit one or more of these sins to unwind. Of course, Satanists do not accept the concept of sin or guilt. They say that man should be free to do whatever he wants to do, as long as his desire does not hurt other people.

Like most cultic groups, Satanists usually believe in some form of reincarnation. Though they do not really believe in either God or Satan, they seem to dread absolute humanism. They believe that in some vague way, the human spirit survives the death of the body and may come back in some other body.

Satanists accuse Christianity of being too soft, with misguided charity toward the weak. They blame Christ for the rise in crime because a society embued with Christian tolerance lacks the backbone to destroy those who need to be destroyed. Some observers have noted a strong echo of Nazism in LaVey's kind of Satanism. Others, including LaVey himself, have drawn parallels between Satanists with their black robes and the Ku Klux Klan with their white robes. Both groups are alienated from traditional society.

Christian concepts of Satan, like their other doctrines, were greatly affected by the Graeco-Roman culture of the early centuries. As it moved into a Gentile world, the church encountered the dualism of gnostic cults. Some of these regarded God and Satan as rival forces, approximately equal, and history as a constant struggle between them. Some of the early Christians toyed with the idea that perhaps Satan was the creator of this world and that Christ's ministry was to rescue man from the evil world that Satan had created.

By the Middle Ages, concepts of the devil had changed radically. By then Satan had become more sensual, more evil. He was no longer merely man's accuser, but man's mortal enemy. The primary symbol of the devil was the goat's head. In popular ideas today the devil still has horns and cloven hoofs. For some reason the goat was firmly associated with evil. The Old Testament speaks of the scapegoat; the New Testament speaks of dividing sheep and goats in judgment. The male goat is also known for his foul odor and unrestrained sexual appetites.

By the late eighteenth century the picture of Satan had changed again. He was no longer the medieval symbol of sexual excess, but a fallen angel more rebellious than wicked. Modern concepts of Satan are greatly influenced by John Milton's *Paradise Lost*, in which Satan is the supreme rebel, self-willed and self-confident, unhumbled in defeat. Milton's devil surveys his lost paradise and says: "To reign is worth ambition though in Hell:/Better to reign in Hell than serve in Heaven." [3]

Most medieval Satan cults were made up of peasants who reacted against the strict teachings of the Catholic Church. It majored on repression, self-denial, and guilt, with an unending dirge of self-rejection. The medieval Church was unsparing in its condemnation of sex, regarded as the worst sin. Clergy were not allowed to marry; virginity was almost deified; and even married couples were taught that sex is inherently evil and to be avoided if at all possible.

In such a repressive atmosphere, it is no wonder that all sorts of emotional and psychological evils resulted. There were outbreaks of witchcraft, demonology, and Satan worship, all with sexual overtones. In Satan cults the peasants rallied around the only symbol they knew for opposition to the Church.

Though the LaVey group is the most familiar, they are by no means the only Satanists in America. The Satanist religion has almost as many varieties as any other denomination. They vary from high-school kids on a lark to middle-aged wife-swapping clubs to misfits assembled to make ritual rejection of a society that has already rejected them.

The Hell's Angels are a motorcycle gang who tear around the country playing Hun and terrorizing people with their mindless cruelty. While genuinely evil, they are only superficially Satanic. They do use some Satanic rituals and symbols, but Satan is more their mascot than master. They are essentially lawless juveniles who get their kicks from group violence.

The Process Church of the Final Judgment is another group with some Satanist overtones. Process members sometimes wear black robes and affect other Satanic ritual and symbols. They believe in one great God, manifest in three forms—Satan, Lucifer, and Jehovah. In Jesus Christ these three are back together after being split up. Most Processeans are young radicals who reject traditional society and its values.

A frightening number of contemporary Satanic cults are truly sinister. Human torture, animal sacrifice, and possibly human murder are being practiced by some of these demented radicals. There were over one hundred murders in California alone between 1965 and 1975 thought to be connected with some occult group or practice. Near Big Sur law officers found several bodies of perfectly skinned dogs, their blood drained. In 1973 and 1974 ranchers in Texas and Oklahoma faced a rash of cattle mutilations in which cattle were killed, their genitals severed, and often their blood completely drained. Most of these cases were never solved, but many officers believe they were connected with weird Satanic groups. Lynette Fromme, one of Manson's witch women, attempted to kill President Ford in 1975.

In 1971 Patrick Newal of Vineland, New Jersey, was pushed to his death at his own request because he was convinced that he would come back as leader of a large Satan pack. A month later an elderly Miami man was stabbed to death by a twenty-two-year-old Satanist who admitted she had greatly enjoyed the stabbing.

For many people, the most horrible expression of Satanism is the infamous "Black Mass." This obscene ritual is a mockery of the Catholic Mass (or Lord's Supper) with all the symbols reversed. It probably originated in the Middle Ages, performed by renegade priests around an altar on which lay a naked prostitute. The wafer symbolizing the Lord's body was subjected to indescribable desecration. A cup containing urine and semen was used for a chalice. The Latin mass was recited backward, invoking Satan instead of Christ. The Black Mass was probably rare, but it did express total rejection of the church and its standards of morality. It often ended with feasting, dancing, laughing, and sexual activities—activities largely forbidden by the medieval church.

The Black Mass has been practiced recently in America, but not as much as many people assume. LaVey is reluctant to perform one. The modern version, while it ridicules Christ and the church, does not approach the vulgar obscenities of the Middle Ages. It has been often commercialized, performed for a fee for curious tourists. One Satanist said the Black Mass is performed today only for those over fifty.

Demons

Millions of Americans lined up to see *The Exorcist*, which portrayed a twelve-year-old girl supposedly possessed by a demon. Audiences watched in delicious horror as the demon gradually took over his victim's personality, turning an innocent child into an obscene, cursing wretch who vomited foul green liquid on the priests who were trying to exorcise her. *The Exorcist* was the rage for months. Sociologists sought to interpret it. Ministers preached sermons on it. Many who viewed the film suffered nightmares afterwards.

What is behind this surprising revival of demonism in our generation? Along with Satanism and witchcraft, belief in demons is a factor to contend with in the weird world of the occult today. While not exactly a religion, belief in demons is definitely a religious phenomenon today.

Demonology is not limited to America. In 1969 five men and women were found guilty in Zurich, Switzerland, of beating a seventeen-year-old girl to death in an effort to drive the devils out of her. Under pressure from her fellow cult members, she confessed to being in league with Satan, who made love to her and promised that one day the two of them would rule the world together. She later died of her injuries.

Belief in invisible demons is one of the oldest ideas of mankind. Historians believe that "trepanned skulls," with holes bored in them, reveal that ancient medicine-men priests tried to relieve suffering patients by drilling a hole in the skull to let the offending demon out. Possibly some of these, by reducing internal pressures, may have relieved suffering, but most such treatments must have been fatal.

According to medieval ideas, demons are frightfully plentiful. They swarm like flies around the birthbed and deathbed, trying to snatch people as they come into the world or leave it. Of course, demons are rarely seen, which just proves how effective they are. Medieval spokesmen figured that about one-third of the hosts of heaven were expelled with Satan at his fall. There were, they said, originally 399,920,004 angels. Those who fell with Satan and became demons amount to 133,306,668, so there are plenty to go around. In Vienna, where Sigmund Freud later practiced his own methods of exorcising psychological demons, in 1583 priests claimed they had cast 12,652 demons out of one sixteen-year-old girl. They later burned the girl's grandmother for good measure, for allegedly keeping several dozen demons around the house in jars.

Demons were (and are) hard to trap because they are masters of disguise. According to tormented medieval people, demons could take the shape of animals, persons, even of Christ himself. One could never know for sure if the faithful dog, the neighbor down the lane, or even the priest who gave out the sacrament might be a demon in disguise. This idea created a kind of medieval *Stepford Wives* syndrome, and many cases are recorded of husbands killing wives, or wives killing husbands, thinking them to be demons. One man killed his young wife because she was so pretty and kind that he knew she must be a demon in disguise.

In ancient times almost all illness was attributed to demons afflicting the body. Demons could cause fever, sores, and of course epilepsy (the very word means "seized upon"). What today would certainly be diagnosed as mental or emotional illness was in the Middle Ages laid off to demons.

Medieval monks attributed the drowsiness that followed the midday meal to the demons of noontime. Demons were also responsible for random trivial thoughts which came unbidden during long prayers and devotions. The simple farmer who, during lengthy prayers by the priest, found himself thinking, "Did I put out feed for the cows?" could be sure that demons were after him. Even up to modern times, practically all suicides were formally attributed to a person's being temporarily overcome by demons. There were demons in the air, in trees, and in water. Even into the twentieth century, some people would make no effort to save a drowning victim because they feared the disappointed water demon would try to claim them next.

Another form of demon was a specialist at sexual encounters. The *incubus* was a male demon who engages in sexual intercourse with a woman; a *succubus* was a female demon who does the same with a man. Thousands of medieval (and some modern) people believed themselves tormented by such demons because of vivid sexual dreams. In more primitive times, children who were retarded or misshapen were often attributed to such unions. This obsession with incubi and succubi probably originated as a way of coping with guilt some people felt at sexual dreams and nocturnal emissions.

Demons could often be identified by their foul odors. After all, their master is called the "unclean spirit." An ancient name for demon is "bog," also slang for latrine. If cleanliness is next to godliness, filthiness is next to demonology. Modern stories like *The Exorcist* make much of detecting a demon's presence by the cold and by foul odors.

One function of demons, apparently, is to make people do things out of character for them, unseemly things they would not ordinarily do. Thus under supposed demon influence, nuns might (and indeed often have) danced nude, respectable matrons have shouted like coarse prostitutes, and mild-mannered men have cursed and raved like brutes.

That there has been a radical revival of interest and belief in demons in recent years cannot be denied. If the American screen and bookshelf can be taken as an indication of what people are thinking, there is a new fascination with demons, devils, and other forms of evil personified.

In the Roman Catholic Church the office of "exorcist" has existed since the early Middle Ages. However, in recent centuries the office has practically disappeared. One might read of one or two exorcisms a decade, mostly in far corners of the earth. However, in the United States there has been a new emphasis upon the training of competent exorcists, and even parish priests are sometimes called on to cast unruly demons out of parishioners. The Catholic Church has been quite cautious, however, refusing to go overboard on modern demonology.

The same cannot always be said for Protestant fundamentalism. Some sensational revivalists have gone to extremes in attributing modern problems to demon possession. Some churches have shown an excessive fascination with demons similar to the superstitions of the Middle Ages. Demon possession plays a central role in cults like the Jesus People, the Children of God, and the modern charismatic movement.

In milder forms, demons may show up as poltergeists, the noisy apparitions that haunt houses and throw things around. They are nuisances, but generally harmless. Some people, like the self-proclaimed witch Sybil Leek, will exorcise houses, businesses, or even entire neighborhoods, sweeping them clean of demons (for a fee).

Contemporary Christians are divided in their interpretation of demons. Many regard them as a real source of spiritual dangers and warn that Christians must watch out lest a demon enter in and possess them at some unsuspecting moment. Other Christians point out that those who believe the Bible are not necessarily obligated to believe in demons today. They also point out that the Bible doctrine of evil, while both real and serious, always involves personal decision. The idea of a demon possessing an innocent child as in *The Exorcist* is foreign to biblical teachings.

However, there can be no doubt that the idea of demons can represent a real threat to Christians. For those who believe them to be real, endless anxiety and fear can result. There is also a moral danger in blaming our sins on some outside force and in failing to face up to our own personal responsibility for our deeds.

Witchcraft

There is a growing fascination in America with ghosts, goblins, and things that go bump in the night. In the zany world of fairies, elves, imps, sprites, vampires, cupids, and leprechauns, it is not surprising that witches are making a comeback. Some contemporary witches are as harmless as the tooth fairy, but others are quite sinister.

In 1976 a North Carolina woman was arrested for possibly causing the death of another woman through witchcraft. The victim had incurred the wrath of Joann Denton, who considers herself a witch. She predicted the elderly woman would die on April 10, 1976, and put various hexes to bring that about. The woman did die on that date, and relatives charged the other woman, alleging that fear contributed to the death.

Television abounds with witches, white and black. Occult book-stores have reams of material about how to practice witchcraft or how to counteract it. Los Angeles has its own official witch, who allegedly conjured up a hex to make the city of the angels more sexy, but called it off when her fee was not paid. In the late 1960s a group of witches attempted to levitate the entire Pentagon nine inches off the ground. I once watched a coven of witches (from a safe distance) as they danced around and mumbled, casting a hex on the Sociology Department of Columbia University.

Modern witches are easy to find because they advertise. You can find them in the yellow pages, not always under "witch," but under such headings as astrology, numerology, or spiritualism. Witches usually meet in covens of thirteen, including six men, six women, and a leader of either sex. This probably originated as a blasphemy of Christ and his twelve apostles. The number is more theoretical than real, for there have always been at least three times as many women witches as men. Some think this may be because women have been deprived of equal rights in ordinary life, and becoming a witch is one way of seeking power.

Most modern witches are young and attractive, like Samantha on *Bewitched*. Crones are definitely out. However, most medieval witches came from the unlovely, unpopular, and rejected elements of society. The ugly, crippled, and grotesque were most likely to be considered witches.

The witches' coven may include housewives, schoolteachers, businessmen, or truck drivers. They hold frequent local meetings (sometimes called "esbats") and usually have thirteen major meetings a year (sometimes called "Sabbats"). Today witches may be white (that is, practicing magic to help people) or black (practicing magic or even Satanism to harm people). People who want to join a coven have to wait until a vacancy occurs. Covens will sometimes loan out a few of their members to train the nucleus of a new coven that is forming.

Some refer to witchcraft as the "Old Religion" and call witches the "Old Ones." They believe that witchcraft is the original religion of nature, never totally displaced by Christianity. In some form, witchcraft dates back to the dawn of history. Original witchcraft was an effort to be in tune with the forces and moods of nature, but medieval witchery took a sinister new turn.

The period from 1450 to 1750 is one of the most desperate in recorded history. Europe was ravaged by the Black Death (bubonic plague), wars, famines, and incredible suffering. During this time of anxiety and insecurity a widespread witchcraft craze first took shape. Many observers point out that in times of crisis, when the fabric of society rips apart, occult forces seem to multiply.

In those desperate times, no doubt many people did consider themselves as witches. Certainly the church and what passed for medicine at that time could not meet their needs. So many people, mostly peasants, turned to whatever powers they could, among which were Satanism, witchcraft, and the dark arts. Most of the medieval witches were women. They rubbed their bodies with what they called "flying ointment," a salve containing aconite and belladonna, which, when rubbed into the skin, act as hallucinogens. Under the influence of this narcotic, the witches thought themselves to fly through the air and gather in large sabbats, where they conjured up tricks and sometimes met the devil. No doubt some actually did attend such meetings.

Suspected witches were tortured and, of course, eventually confessed whatever the inquisitors wanted. These "confessions" were recorded in lurid detail, providing a guide to other witch groups who actually tried to practice what others had simply fabricated.

The medieval Catholic Church moved militantly to suppress the horde of witches who threatened to engulf them. In 1484 the church issued an official condemnation of witchcraft and allowed inquisitors almost unchecked powers to question, torture, and execute witches on what today would be considered the flimsiest evidence. Two years later saw publication of *Malleus Maleficarum* (The Hammer of Witches), which was to become the bible of witch-hunting for several centuries. This desperate document says witches can cause cows to go dry, make men impotent and women barren, fly through the air on brooms, and make children break out with rashes.

Not only could witches destroy crops; they could also switch entire fields, so that a man with a good fertile field might later find it turned by witchcraft into barren, lifeless soil. It was far easier to attribute such soil deterioration to witchcraft than to erosion, lack of fertilizer, and lack of crop rotation. According to the *Malleus Maleficarum*, witches had a special ability to turn themselves into animals, especially cats. They also took special delight in harming farm animals, which came to be known as "stable witchcraft."

Torture was specifically allowed to prove witchcraft. For example, when a violent hailstorm destroyed crops at Constance, the townspeople demanded that the church launch an investigation. It turned out that two women (witches, of course) had caused the hailstorm. One of them confessed after only "the gentlest questions, being suspended hardly clear of the ground by her thumbs."

From ancient times witches, like fairies, had been mysterious, capricious, semisupernatural beings with magical powers. Usually they did no harm unless provoked. However, one result of the *Malleus* was to firmly link witchcraft with allegiance to Satan. Thus witchcraft became a heresy as well as a crime. Modern witchcraft is no longer exclusively linked with Satan and evil. The so-called white witches represent a reversion to the older superstitions of the harmless or even benevolent witch.

Some estimate that up to two million may have been put to death in the medieval witch purge. Most of these were women, but possibly 20 percent were men; and a surprising number were children. However, the milder judges did not always execute the children of witches. Often it was considered enough to beat them half to death and brand them on the forehead so they could be watched for any signs of following in Mother's footprints.

The most familiar case of witchcraft in America was at Salem, Massachusetts, in 1692. In that strict Puritan village adolescent girls led a sudden outbreak of witchery, accusing various citizens of "tormenting" them. The girls, ranging in age from nine to eighteen, would twitch, writhe, groan, and scream out. Frantic parents, pastors, and judges were quick to buy the witchcraft explanation. Within a few months 150 people were arrested. Thirty-one were tried, and twenty-one persons and one dog were put to death for practicing witchcraft. Then, almost as suddenly as it began, the horrible thing ended with a sobered panel of judges confessing their haste in executing honorable citizens on insufficient evidence.

A staple in the Salem witchcraft trials was what was called "spectral evidence." Most of those accused by the girls of coming to torment them by night could and did give alibis, with witnesses, of being elsewhere at the time. However, this was irrelevant because it was well known that the Devil could assume the "spectral shape" of one of his followers. Thus a person could be held responsible for what the Devil did while borrowing his body. Of course, there is absolutely no defense against this kind of "evidence."

One of the Salem "witches" was a young widow who ran a boardinghouse, causing two opinion strikes against her before the trial ever began in this repressive Puritan community. To make matters worse, she was young and attractive and wore a form-fitting red blouse. Several of the men testified that her spectral shape came to their minds at night and tormented them. She was forthwith pronounced a witch.

At Salem, as always, witchcraft flourished at times of crisis in society. In 1691-92 the Salem people faced smallpox epidemics, Indian uprisings, and unusually poor crops. The small community of Puritans had their full share of problems. Perhaps one reason for the upsurge of witchcraft, as well as other occult superstititions, is that people feel powerless to cope with the crises around them. One Salem citizen, skeptical about witchcraft, said, "Witches indeed. Let me change but one letter and I will explain them all."

What is behind the modern revival of witchcraft? One would hardly expect the most highly educated generation in history to eagerly embrace the world's oldest superstition, but that is happening. There can be no doubt that America is on a major spiritual revolution. The old values are crumbling, as are the institutions that embody them. The modern chrome-plated god of science threatens to destroy us. People without Christ are empty, without a sense of values or spiritual reality. No longer able to believe in the traditional religions, many have turned to witches, demons, and even Satan to fill the void in their lives.

Is witchcraft real? You can get a disagreement on that question in almost any group. However, it is obvious that the *effects* of witchcraft are real for those who believe in it. People who believe that hexes are powerful tend to get sick if they know a hex has been put on them. So it is possible for witchcraft to be powerful, whether or not there is any objective reality behind it.

Conclusion

Satan worship, demonology, and witchcraft are but three forms in which modern occult beliefs are expressed. There are many mysteries for a Christian, but one thing is sure: the person who holds fast to Jesus Christ has nothing to fear from any being, spirit, principality, or "thing" in the entire universe. Jesus Christ is Lord.

References

1. Anton S. LaVey, *The Satanic Bible* (New York: Avon Books, 1969), p. 23.
2. Arthur Lyons, *The Second Coming: Satanism in America* (New York: Dodd, Mead and Co., 1970), p. 173.
3. Richard Cavendish, *The Powers of Evil* (New York: G. P. Putman's Sons, 1975), p. 225.

For Further Reading

Holzer, Hans. *The Truth About Witchcraft.* New York: Doubleday and Co., Inc., 1969.
Newport, John P. *Demons, Demons, Demons.* Nashville: Broadman Press, 1972.

Philpott, Kent. *A Manual of Demonology and the Occult.* Grand Rapids: Zondervan Publishing House, 1973.
Smith, Susy. *Today's Witches.* Englewood Cliffs, N.J.: Prentice-Hall, Inc., 1970.

8. Understanding the New Religions

Probing Beneath the Surface

Like a 33 RPM record playing at 78 RPM, things seemed to speed up during the 1960s. Of course, religious ideas and groups have always been subject to change; but in recent years the change has reached runaway stage. Ideas that had endured for centuries crumbled overnight. Like a farmer who can no longer recognize his own field for the strange new plants springing up everywhere, Americans are now reaping a bumper crop of strange new religions. Some of them are brand new. Others are strange hybrids or blends of earlier religions. Some are old plants, long dormant, which have sprung to life again as the spiritual climate shifted.

In these chapters we have sought to throw a spotlight on several of these new religions that are springing up all around us. The approach has been descriptive, to show briefly how each group originated, what they stand for, and how they carry on their activities. This concluding chapter turns away from the individual trees to try to bring the entire forest into focus. We will look at the larger context of the new religions and raise questions about their overall significance.

We might begin by asking, Why here? Why now? Why should these new religions spring up in the 1960s and 1970s and not in the 1920s or 1930s? Why, after unbroken centuries of facing West, has American religion turned Eastward with such fascination? Why has the most scientific age in history turned with such passion to rank superstition? How does it happen that in the generation that devised sophisticated computers, so many make their decisions by Tarot cards?

To understand the new religions, we must see them in social context. They are profoundly influenced by the environment out of which they come and, in turn, provide a valuable commentary upon that environment. Taken separately, perhaps no one of these new religions represents more than a footnote in history. But taken together, they represent a fundamental shift in twentieth-century American religion.

An Explosion of New Religions

Organized religions, like oak trees, take a long time to grow. Unless you count Communism or secularism as religions, no major world religion has been born since Mohammedanism in the seventh century. But suddenly, in little over a decade, we have witnessed an explosion of new cults and sects unlike anything in history.

The cults examined in this book are merely one fraction of the tip of the iceberg. In addition to major Protestant, Catholic, and Jewish denominations, no one knows how many new religious cults exist in America. Some estimate the figure at several hundred, with the number of members well into the millions.

The confusing variety of new cults can be illustrated just by naming a few not included in this book, such as the Bo Peep group, Full Moon Meditation groups, the Giant Rock Space Convention, the Amalgamated Flying Saucer Clubs, the Gurdjieff groups, the Prosperos, Abilitism, Builders of the Adytum, Feraferia, the Satya Sai Baba Movement, the Baba Lovers, the Nichiren Shoshu of America, the Subud, Guru Maharaj Ji and the Divine Light Mission, and Cargo Cults.

Each of these and hundreds more like them are winning disciples in the shadow of our churches. And these are examples of the *new* groups, to say nothing of older cults like Theosophy, Rosicrucianism, Baha'i, New Thought, and Spiritualism. The result has been to turn America into a confusing spiritual smorgasbord in which every imaginable religious recipe is not only available, but clamors for acceptance.

Many of the new religions have a "floating population" of samplers who drift in and out. Those who are presently "into"

Zen may previously have been into something else and may shortly move on to still other gurus. It would be too harsh to say that people conditioned to accept one absurdity find the next one easier to take, but some observers have said just that. At present there is no evidence that the emergence of new religions is abating. Apparently the trend has not yet run its course, and indications are that probably still more new religions will spring up between the time I write these words and you read them.

What's Behind the New Religions?

Why have the new religions risen? What are the forces, social and religious, that have called them into existence?

We can rarely say for *sure* why anything happened. We may pinpoint probable causes, but some mystery remains. No human motive is entirely pure or clear, so we can at times only guess why people do what they do.

You have probably heard forecasts in which the weatherman reported that conditions were right for a tornado to develop. This does not mean that tornadoes *always* form at such times, but that all the ingredients are present. Similarly, the turbulent and unstable social conditions of the 1960s and since have allowed new religions to spawn.

Look first at the social factors which midwived the new religions. The 1960s brought disillusionment, especially among the young, unmatched in our history. In 1963 alone, we saw JFK gunned down in Dallas, four mop-haired English youths called Beatles introduce a cultural as well as musical revolution among the young, Harvard professor Timothy Leary pronounce LSD as a substitute for religion, and the Supreme Court underscore American secularism by a ruling which many saw as outlawing prayer in public schools.

The Great Society never quite came off, and we lost the war on poverty as well as the war in Vietnam. The Civil Rights Movement of brotherhood died with its martyred leader, Martin Luther King, to reemerge as the militant Black Power movement. The fires of Watts revealed rotting cities, alienated rural areas, and frightened suburbs. To ward off its critics the government itself became corrupt, as Watergate was to reveal later.

Modern science "explained" the universe, leaving neither mystery nor wonder. Then, like a cosmic Frankenstein, science turned on its creators, threatening disaster by plastic litter, industrial pollution, chemical poisons, or nuclear holocaust. It is no wonder that "technocracy's children," as Roszak calls them, turned away from the "bastard god science." What better way to reject science than by turning to astrology? There is no more pointed way to snub the computer than by relying on Tarot cards or I Ching.

What Petersen called "future fright" also played a role. Young people heard so much of population explosion, nuclear threat, and pollution crisis that they doubted if there would be a future. In such a world, should they take security in the eternal Now of Eastern mysticism? Or should they perhaps give up on the world and look eagerly for Armageddon?

Perhaps no social factor contributed more to the new religions than did family disintegration. The dismal evidence cannot be cited here, but mobility, working mothers, more sexual freedom, and the generation gap took a frightful toll on the American family. The one last bastion in a lonely world where one could be sure of his status slipped away. It is more than incidental that practically all of the new religions seek in some way to provide a substitute for the family.

Widespread drug usage was both a cause and a symptom of the alienated subculture that fed into the new religions. The high priest of the chemical satori, Timothy Leary, said, "The LSD kick is spiritual ecstasy. The LSD trip is a religious pilgrimage." [1] Users reached altered states of consciousness via drugs, taking a chemical shortcut to the goal offered by Eastern religions. For many, drugs proved the entranceway to Eastern religions like Zen and Krishna, and to a lesser extent TM. When John Lennon sang in "I Am the Walrus" that "I am he as you are me and we are all together," he was expressing not only drug hallucination, but also the deepest theology of Eastern religions, namely the ultimate merging of the self with the universe.

Religious factors also prepared the way for the new religion explosion. Organized religion shared many of the same ills as society—indeed, had contributed some of them. Traditional Protestant, Catholic, and Jewish religions were not meeting the spiritual needs of many young people, or at least youth did not *think* their needs were being met, which amounts to the same thing. This created a market for new religious suppliers.

Sydney Ahlstrom suggests that 1960 marked the end of four hundred years of Puritan influence, dating from the coronation of Queen Elizabeth I. The WASP culture of Puritan Protestantism dominated America during that time, he suggests, but we now witness the breakup of the Puritan synthesis.[2] We have entered a new chapter of the religious history of America.

During these years, many criticisms have been leveled at the traditional churches. They are accused of self-interest, of being more concerned for their own institutional survival than for the needs of people. Some say the church has so emphasized the individual as to lose sight of the group, allowing the Greek heritage of individualism to dominate the Hebrew-Christian emphasis upon community. Others accuse the church of concentrating on such a narrow spirituality (saving "souls") that they have neglected the biblical message about life, the body, and work in this world.

Young people are often put off by the "not now" attitude of the church. The church points to the *past*, when God did marvelous things, and promises a *future* when we shall see face to face; but it has often been short on the *now*. This poverty of the present has conditioned many young people to opt for the new religions, many of which have no interest in past or future, but promise meaningful religious experiences right now. Zen Buddhism, for example, likes to call itself the Now Religion.

Perhaps a more serious accusation is that the church has been long on message, but short on method. We have preached ideas, concepts, and explanations; but, as critics maintain, we rarely show people how to *do* the Christian life. One drawing card of the new religions is that they come on with a specific technique, method, or discipline and say, *This is how to do it*. The important thing is not *what* the method is, whether sitting sazen with the Zennists or chanting with the Krishnas, but that it is clear, definite, and has a guru or master to give demonstrations that can serve as a model.

A surprising number of the new religions begin in California. Some say California is not as much a state as it is a state of mind. The sun, surf, and Hollywood have drawn people westward like a magnet, many of them young. In this westward trek the "pieties of the plains" either dried up on the desert or survived with desert intensity. Needleman suggests that California, unlike most of America, has at last left behind the European heritage, both religious and intellectual.[3] This absence of binding tradition gives freedom to explore new religious forms. Perhaps no other city in the world has such an amazing variety of religions, new and old, as does Los Angeles.

Major Motifs of the New Religions

Each new religion has its own guru, its own scripture text, and its own distinctive corner of the theological market. Despite their differences, however, some common patterns emerge.

A new kind of religion.—Ellwood suggests there are two basic *kinds* of religion, that built around "cosmic wonder" and that grounded in "revelation."[4] Religions of cosmic wonder are little concerned with history and are communicated by "exemplary" leaders who are *models* rather than messengers. Religions of revelation, however, believe God works in history and are communicated by "emissary" leaders who come with a *message* from God. Cosmic religions look for God *within*, whereas revelational religions look for God to reveal himself to man from *without*. Judaism, Christianity, and Mohammedanism are religions of historical revelation, whereas Hinduism and Buddhism are religions of cosmic wonder. Most of the new religions in America follow the Eastern pattern.

After centuries of neglect, America is once again open to the East. The Korean and Vietnam wars caused us to look eastward; some suggest that the admission of Hawaii to statehood also reminded us that the East exists. Certainly in recent years it has been impossible to ignore that one-fourth of humanity called China.

Many people forget that Christianity originated as an Eastern religion and that in early centuries, its theology and spiritual styles were influenced by the East. Practices like meditation, satori, ecstasy, and forsaking the world, often identified with Eastern religions, have an authentic heritage also in Christianity.

This open window toward the East may have a long-range impact upon Western religion. One observer said, "We sense a new spiritual type emerging in contemporary America. The new spiritual man is more like the kind of person we have heretofore associated with the East—or with cultists. He presumes without question that God or spiritual reality, if it is to be found, is to be found within through expanded states of consciousness which penetrate like searchlights toward the deep floor of being. Inner exploration is his main concern." [5]

New sources of authority.—The new religions are unimpressed by the Bible, and creeds they dismiss as irrelevant. Most of them depend upon their own experience as their only religious authority. They are little interested in words, creeds, or sermons. "May the Baby Jesus open your mind and shut your mouth," one cultist said. Nor do most of them reflect upon their experience or do much comparing of their experience with that of others. Raw experience is their only guide.

Those who accept some form of written authority generally displace the Bible in favor of their own new scriptures. The Mo-letters of the Children of God and the *Divine Principle* of the Moonies are examples.

Disengagement from the world.—One of the oldest problems facing Christians is their relation to the world. Early Christians looked for the end of the world; medieval monks withdrew from the world into monasteries. Modern Protestants generally participate in the world as part of their Christian duty.

The new religions, however, are less interested in the outer world. Their concern is not to subdue the earth, but to subdue themselves. Some of the new cults look eagerly for the end of the world, revealing their despair and hostility by their eschatology. Others merely ignore the world, while some deny its existence.

If the new religions prevail, who is to bear a meaningful witness to the world? Who will point out moral and ethical issues in the political, economic, and social realms? Christians are to be in the world, but not of it. This suggests a delicate balance that we have not always observed.

New practices in marriage and sex.—Puritan sex and monogamous marriage are under heavy attack today. The nuclear family, we are told, is breaking down and probably ought to, for it cannot carry the heavy load our society has assigned it. Our generation, we are informed, will probably be the last to marry in the traditional sense. The end of marriage, like the end of the world, has been predicted more often than it has happened.

Most of the new religions have some new scheme for marriage, sex, and the family. Some seek to ration sex, as some Moonies and Hare Krishnas. Others allow sexual freedom, including concubinage and some form of group marriage. Almost all the new religions seek to form some version of the larger family, and many of them intentionally break down the nuclear or "diminished" family. However, many of them still hold to some version of male dominance.

Perhaps Christianity has through the years absorbed unwholesome ideas on sex and marriage from the surrounding society. The early church confronted gnostic and dualistic philosophy, which despised the body and regarded sex as evil. By the time of Augustine, sin had become a three-letter word spelled s-e-x. The medieval church taught contempt for sex, even within marriage, and almost deified virginity (as in the Virgin Mary). When the Puritan repressions were added to this medieval rejection of sex, it became even more difficult for Christians to hear the biblical message that God created men and women for each other. Sex within marriage is one of God's most winsome gifts. The new religions may do traditional Christianity a favor if they help them recover the wholesome, honest earthiness of the Bible.

Reaction against permissiveness.—Authority is strict in most of the new religions as far as life-style and community organization. Freedom to inquire, freedom to disagree, and freedom to grant truth in diverse traditions are notably lacking. Most of them have a strong leader, elected or self-appointed, to whom the group must be obedient. Of course, there are degrees of freedom, from the coarse coercion of the Children of God to the subtle brainwashing of the Moonies.

Perhaps in reaction to the devastating permissiveness of the 1960s, some of the new cults are disturbingly authoritarian. In some, obedience has become blind. A similar trend is seen in some traditional churches, where Bill Gothard's *Institute of Basic Youth Conflicts* sells the same form of unthinking obedience found in many of the cults. Those who accept this message must sell out their own freedom and responsibility as persons, but they gain the emotional security and reassurance of the group.

Forms of ecstasy.—Most of the new religions engage in some form of altered consciousness or ecstasy. The belief persists that we can shift mental gears and flash different kinds of film on our spiritual screen. Ecstasy in the new religions takes many forms. Some achieve it by drugs, others by meditation, by sitting zazen, by trance, or by speaking in tongues.

By these means they escape the "ordinariness of life" and validate their religious experience. Some form of ecstatic utterance or unknown tongues has marked every major religion, dating at least as far back as the Delphic Oracles, centuries before Christ.

Irrationality.—Like Tertullian, who said *credo quia impossible* (I believe because it is absurd), many of the new cultists make a virtue of the senseless and irrational. Irrational teachings are no barrier to belief, as we see in witchcraft, cargo cults, and other strange new ventures. In fact, some of the new cults seem drawn to non-sense, having rejected rationality per se.

Perhaps this rejection of "meaning" in its traditional sense is a reaching for a higher meaning in wonder, magic, and mystery— in short, a reaching beyond meaning to transcendence.

Pelagian theology.—To the extent they have a theology, most of the new religions are Pelagian in their doctrine of man. That is, they assume the basic goodness, or at least potential goodness, of man. Even the superfundamentalists, like the Children of God, believe that while the world is wicked, they at least are good. Man has unlimited potential for good, man can be in touch with God, man and God at the highest levels merge into one—these statements sum up the views of many of the new groups, especially those of an Eastern bent.

There is no serious facing up to man's potential for evil in the new cults. Man merely needs some method of technique to release the good *that is inherent within him.* Few of them have any concept of a redeemer from without, such as Jesus Christ.

How to Witness to the New Religions

How to bear a Christian witness to the new cults is one of the toughest questions around. Tracts like "How to Witness to a Mormon" or "Witnessing to Jehovah's Witnesses" suggest just what to say, what Scriptures to quote, and what arguments to advance. Most of these are useless.

The unwelcome truth is that in many cases we cannot witness effectively to the fanatic cults, and all efforts to do so are a waste of time. Most of our witnessing has been to lead a person who basically believes in Christ to act upon that belief and accept him as Savior. Most of us are not adept or experienced in dealing with people, like members of the new religions, who reject Christianity, God, the Bible, and the Hebrew-Christian world view.

Some Christians ignore the cults, while others go to the opposite extreme of a harsh (and perhaps illegal) process of "deprogramming." The following suggestions fall somewhere between these extremes.

Preventive witness is probably best. If Christians can identify the spiritual needs the new cults address and can see to it that their own churches meet those needs, there will be less room for the cults. People want identity, status, and loving acceptance in a meaningful group. The church can and should provide solutions to those needs. But if it does not, people will find them elsewhere. As in treating disease, we need to get behind the symptoms to the causes. If Christians can deal with the disillusionment that feeds the cults, there will be less occasion to try to win back the cult members.

In witnessing to the cults, there is little value in arguing from meaningless bases. The Christian gains little by pointing out that the cult is irrational. Pointing out that his teaching is in conflict with the Bible will mean little to one who rejects the Bible. However, this might be an effective witness to a Christian youth who is considering joining a cult.

Dealing with the "hard-core" brainwashing cults presents other problems. We may ultimately come to some sort of government restriction if it is proven that their practices are illegal or harmful. In the meantime, for people victimized by such cults, some limited form of deprogramming may be necessary as a last resort. However, this approach should be in the hands of experienced experts who demonstrate restraint and integrity.

Perhaps the best witness is to allow Christ and his grace to permeate our lives. We can show that Christ really does meet spiritual needs.

Conclusion

America is now a land of religious pluralism. Christianity has competition; the days of religious monopoly are gone. This means we must adjust our strategy to win disciples in the open market of religious variety.

This is an exciting time to live. The past quarter-century will go down as one of the most religious times in American history. People are asking religious questions, seeking ultimate meaning. This fact affords Christians a great opportunity to win the hearts and minds of people.

References

1. William J. Petersen, *Those Curious New Cults* (New Canaan, Connec-

ticut: Keats Publishing Co., 1975), p. 14.
2. Sydney E. Ahlstrom, *A Religious History of the American People* (New Haven: Yale University Press, 1972), p. 1079.
3. Jacob Needleman, *The New Religions* (New York: Doubleday and Co., Inc., 1970), p. 3.
4. Robert S. Ellwood, Jr., *Religious and Spiritual Groups in Modern America* (Englewood Cliffs, N.J.: Prentice-Hall, Inc., 1973), p. xiv.
5. Ibid., pp. xiv-xv, emphasis added.

For Further Reading

Bach, Marcus, *Spiritual Breakthroughs for Our Time.* New York: Doubleday and Co., Inc., 1965.
McNamara, Patrick H., ed. *Religion American Style.* New York: Harper and Row, Publishers, 1974.
Roszak, Theodore. *The Making of a Counter Culture.* New York: Doubleday and Co., Inc., 1969.